# INTERGALACTIC TRIP STOP

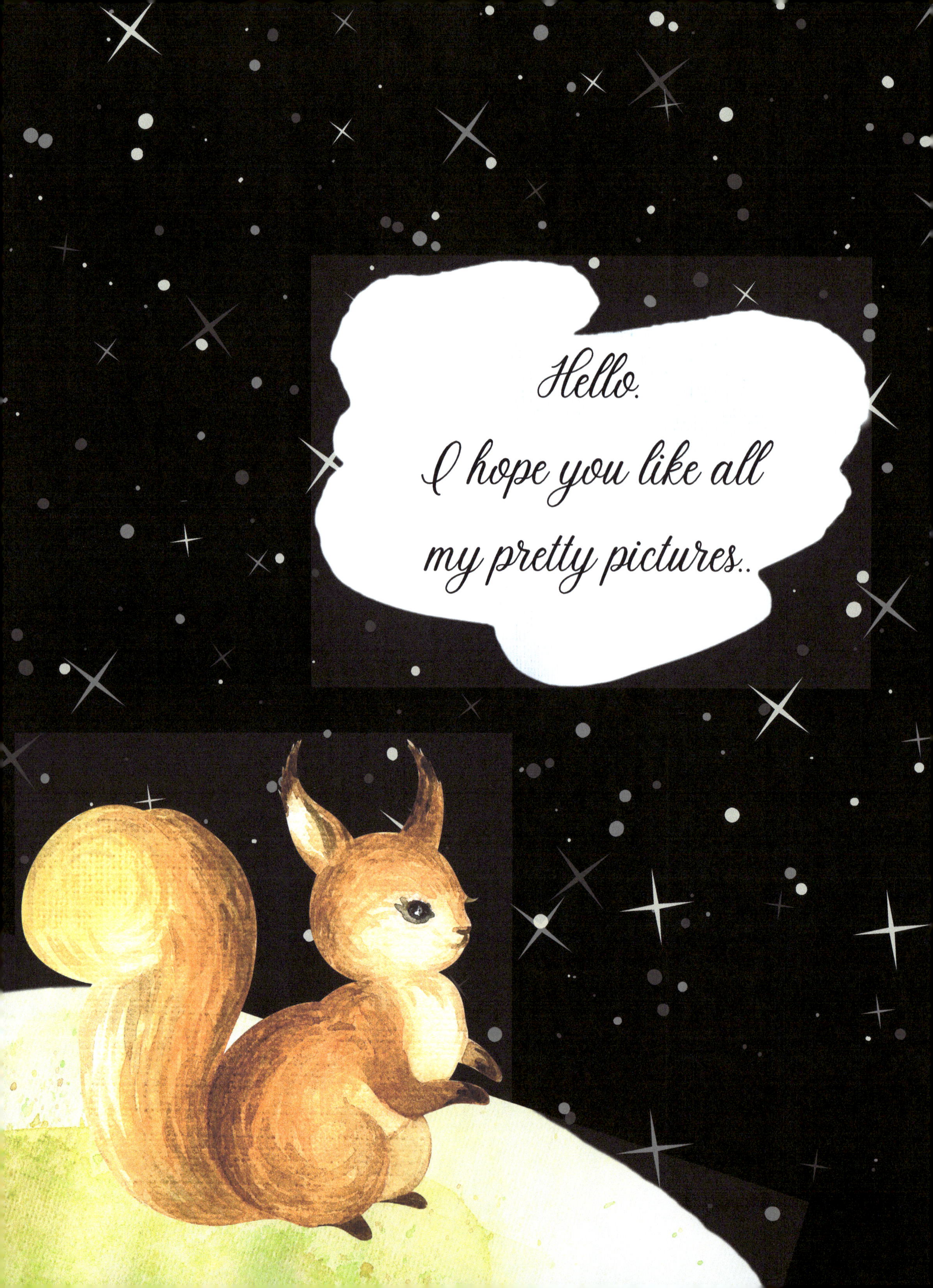
Hello.
I hope you like all
my pretty pictures..

Take a look.

And have a beautiful trip.

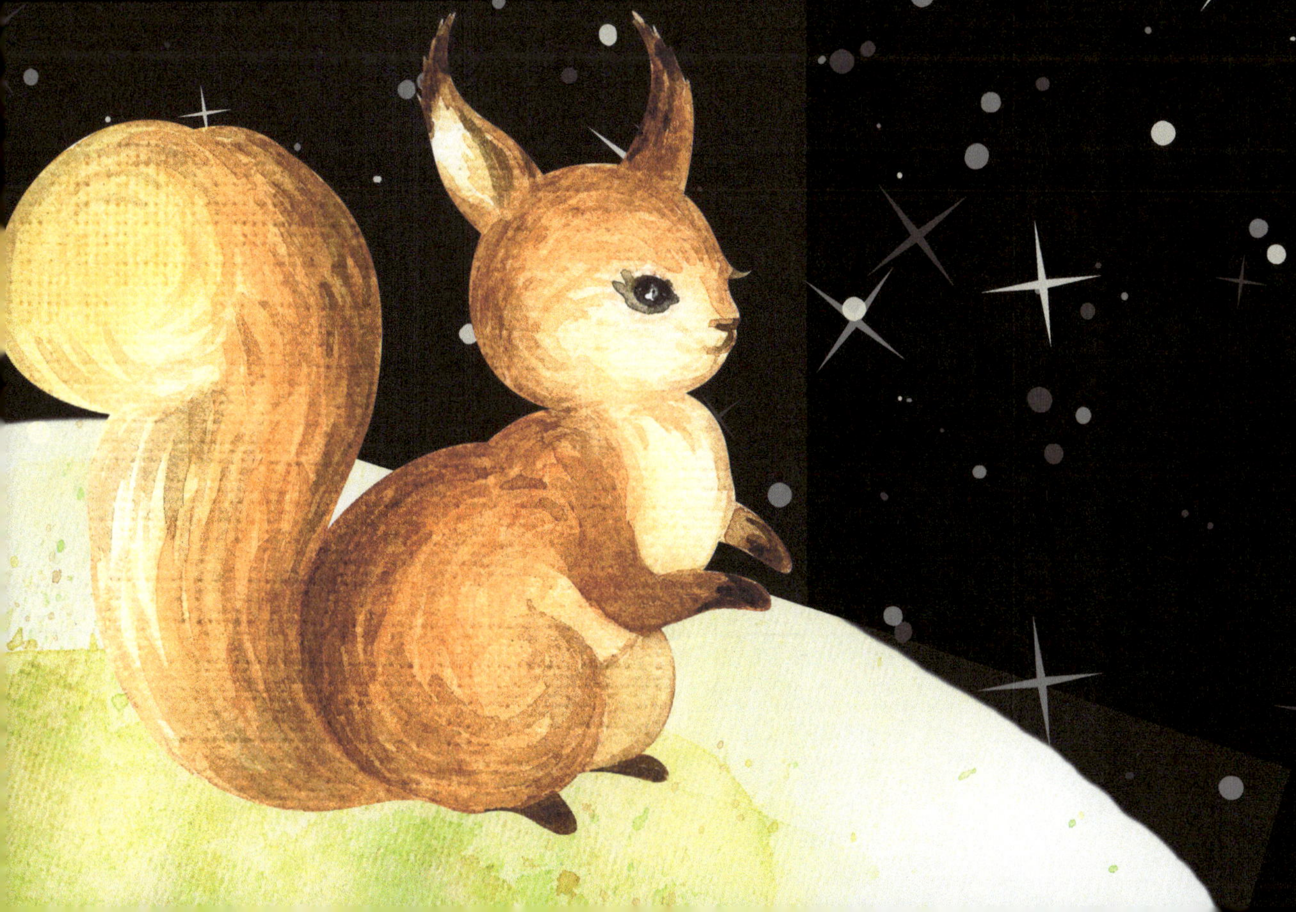

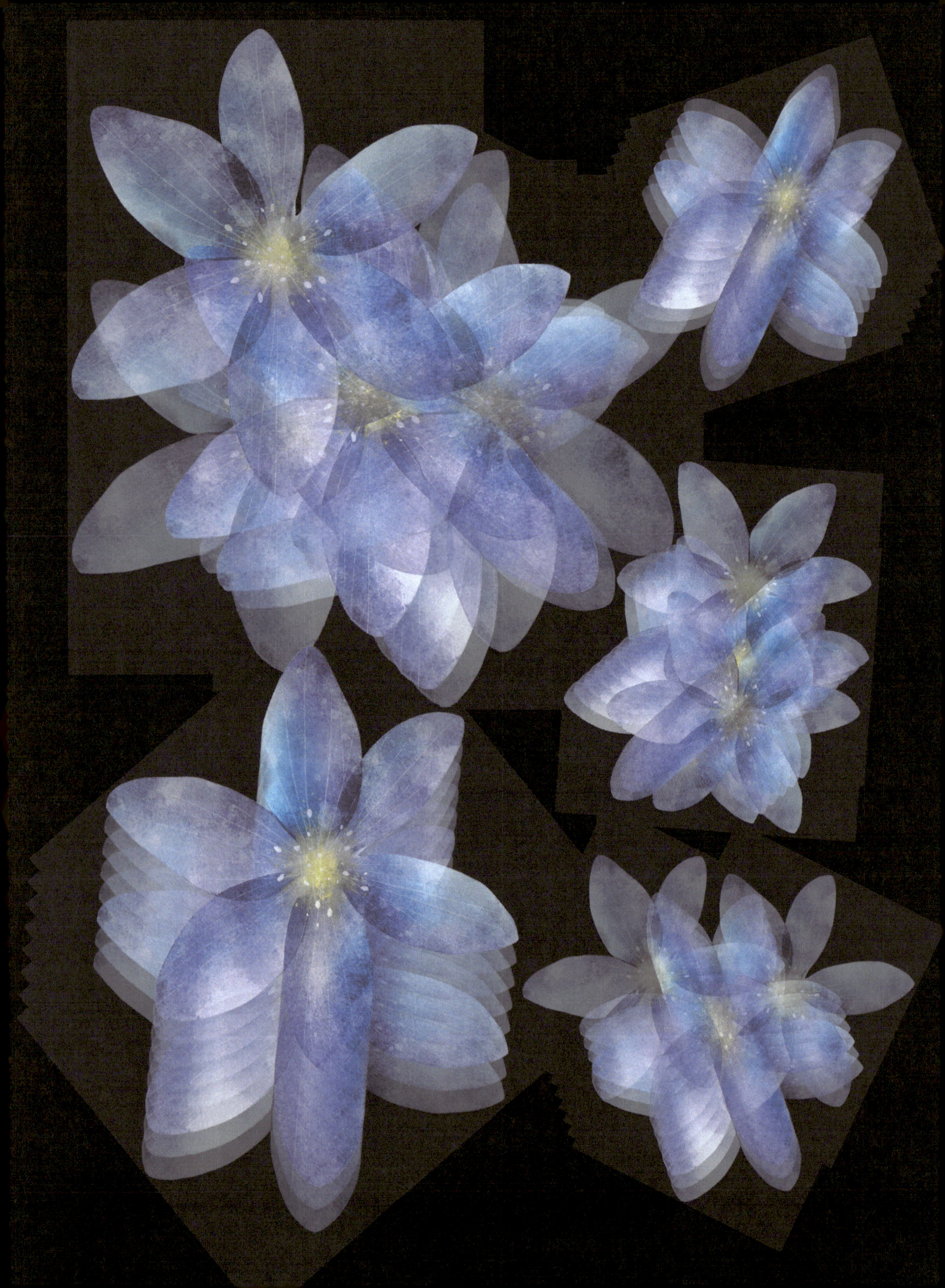

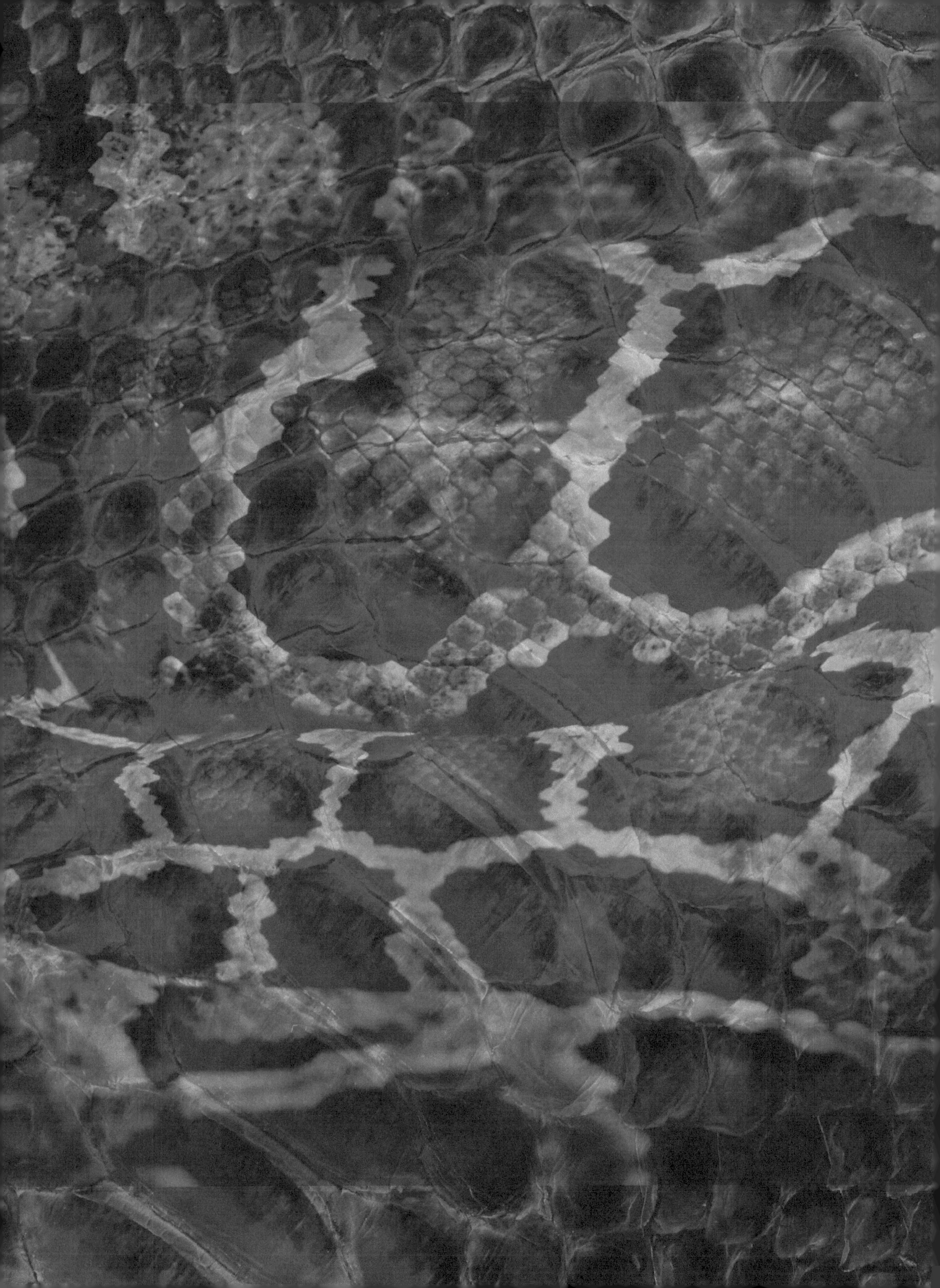

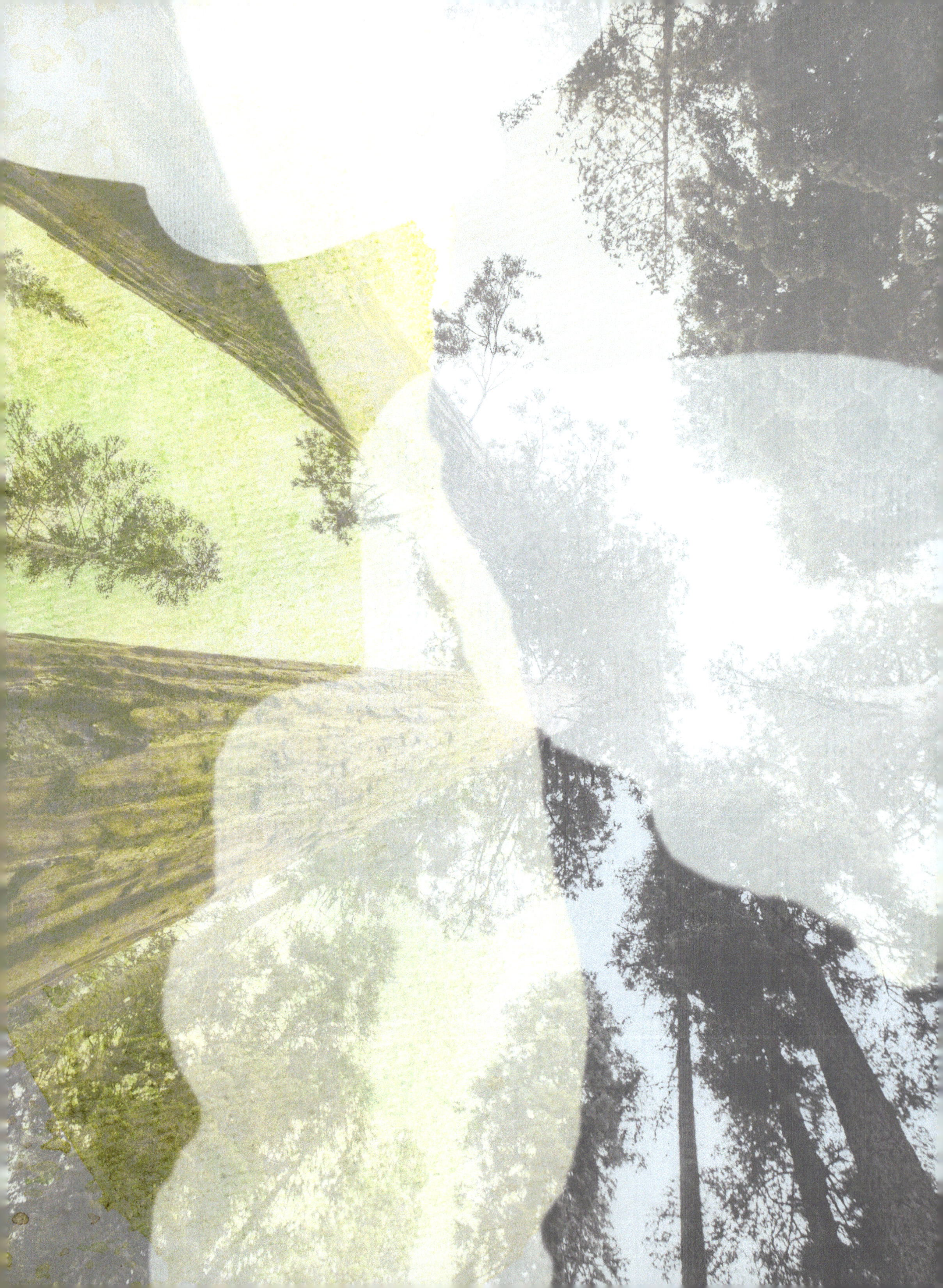

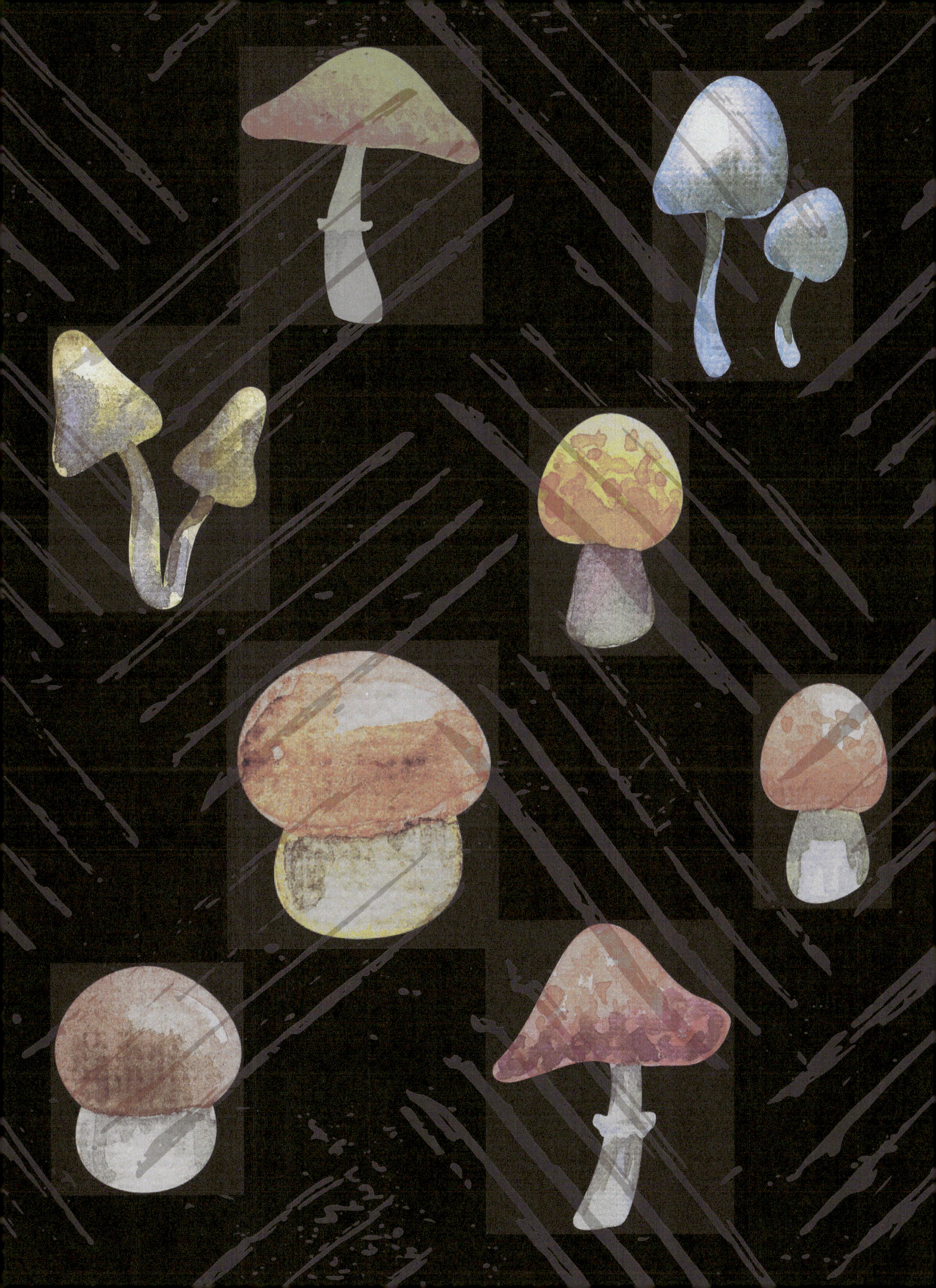

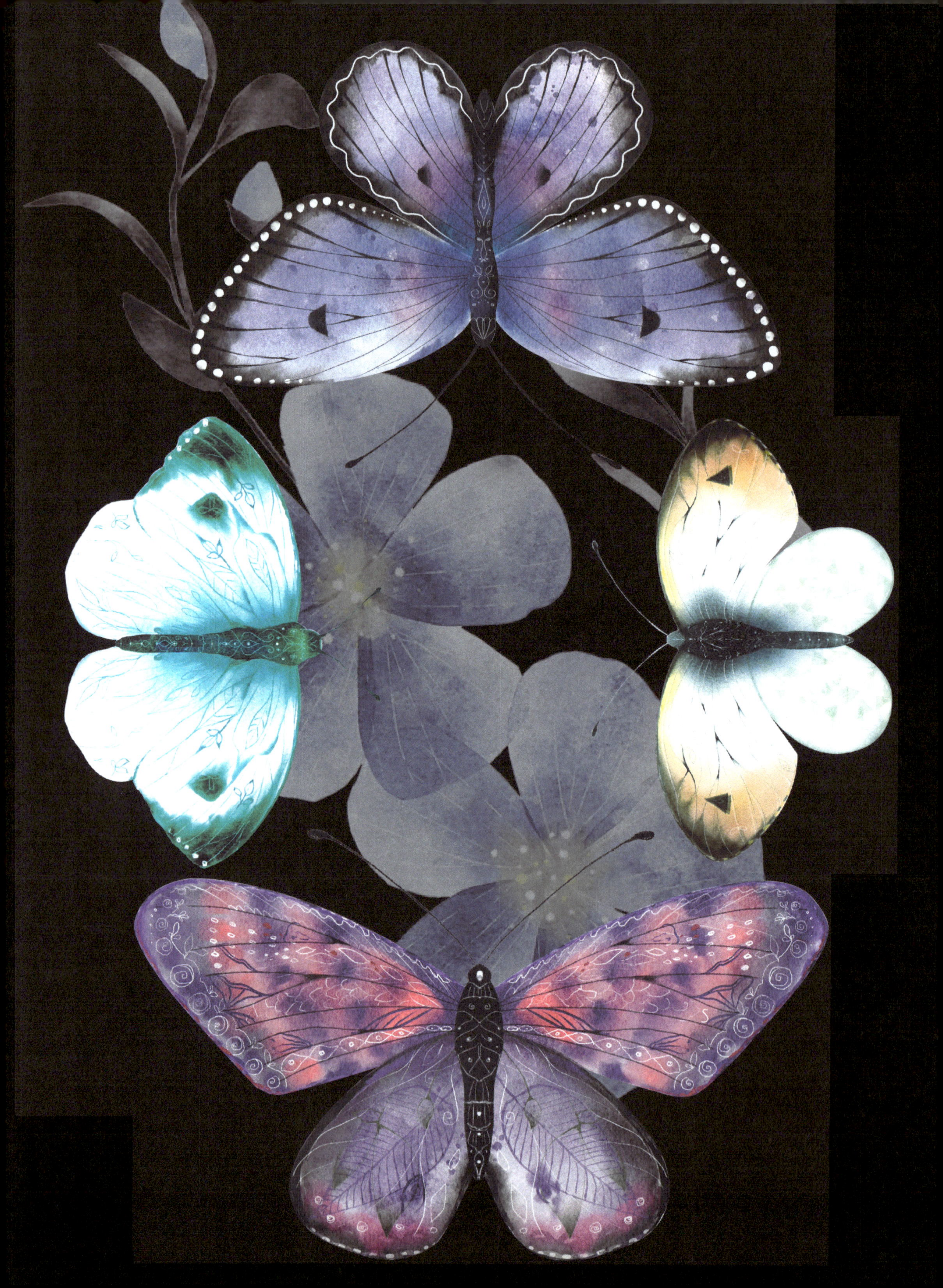

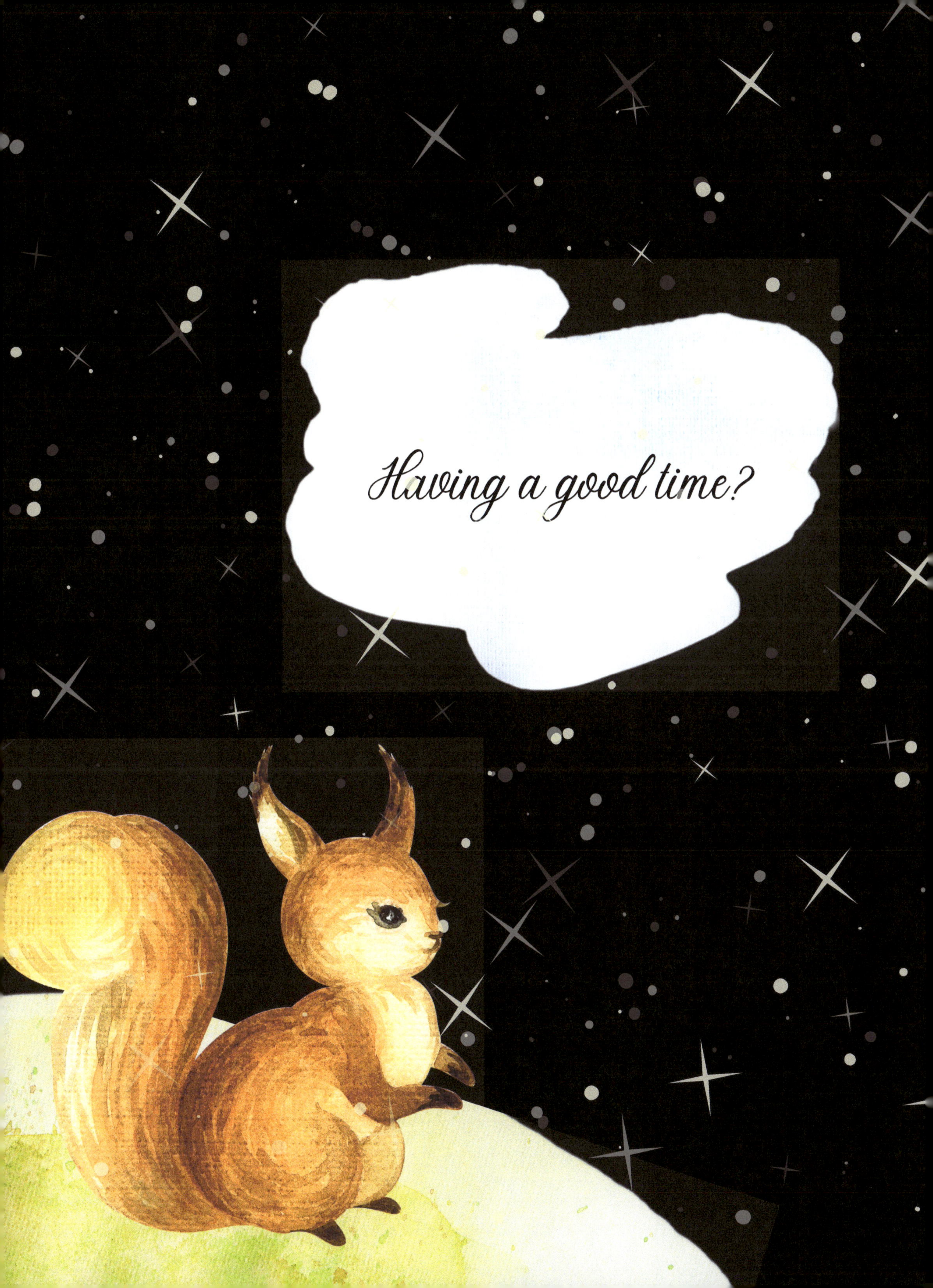
Having a good time?

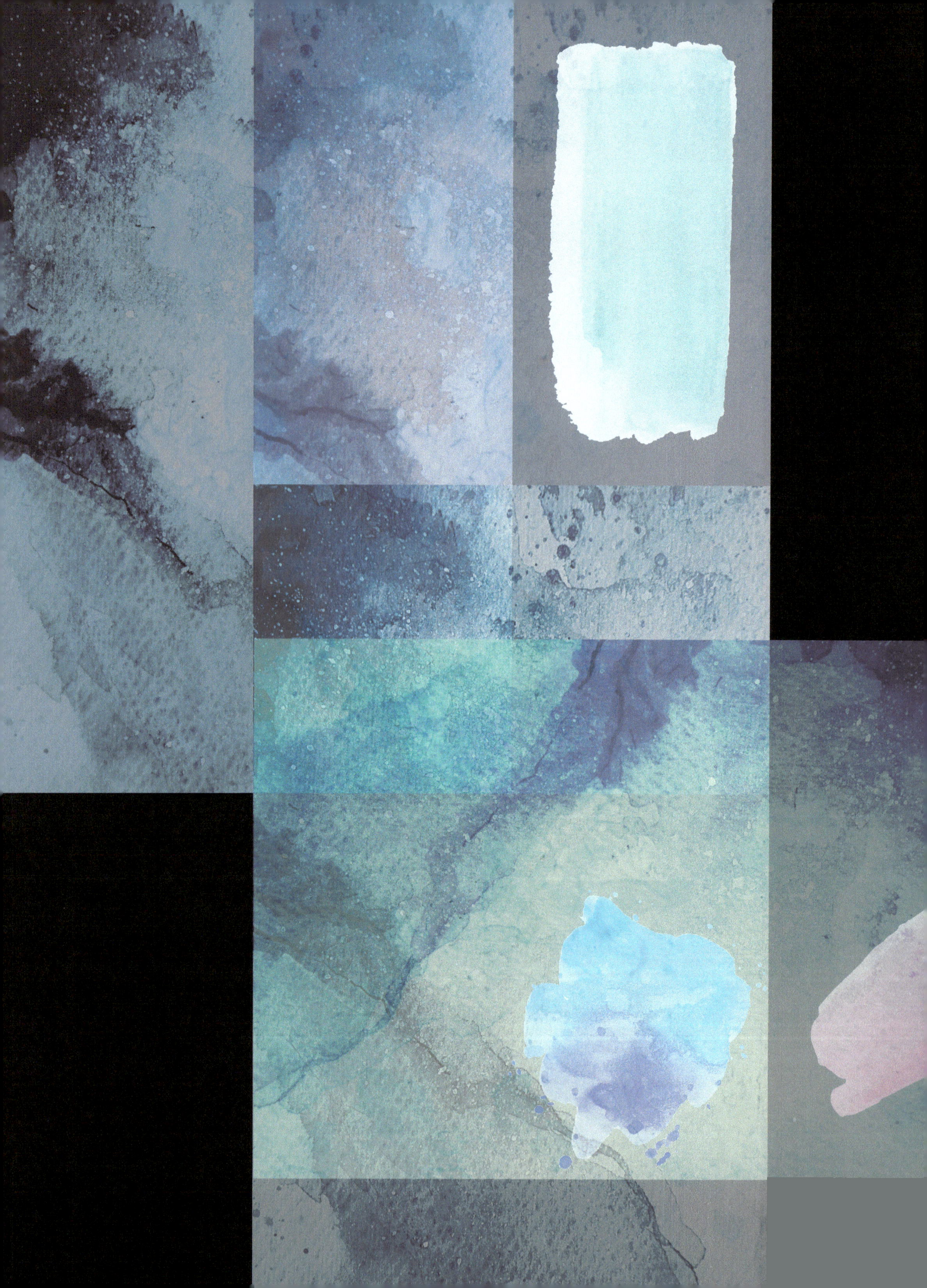

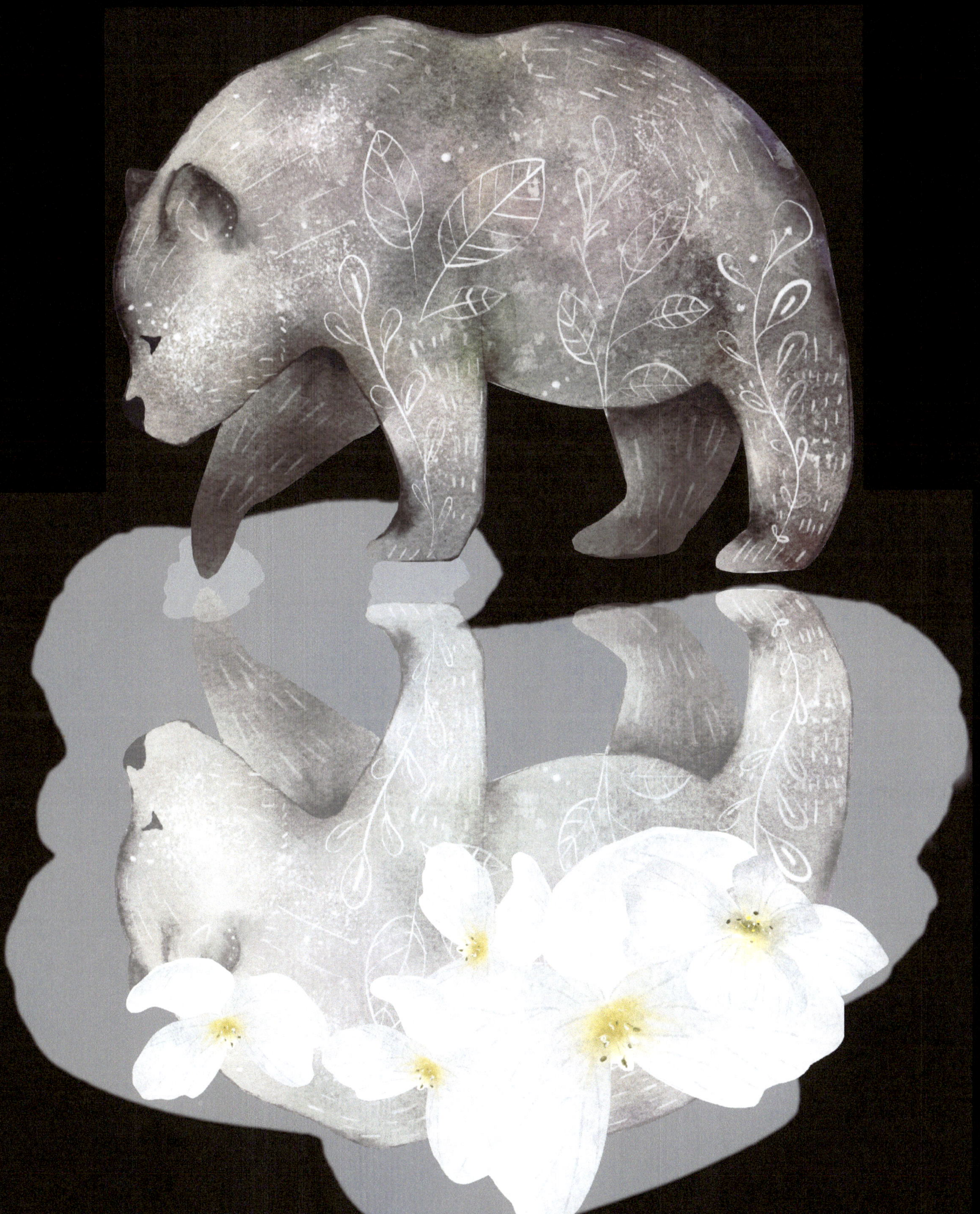

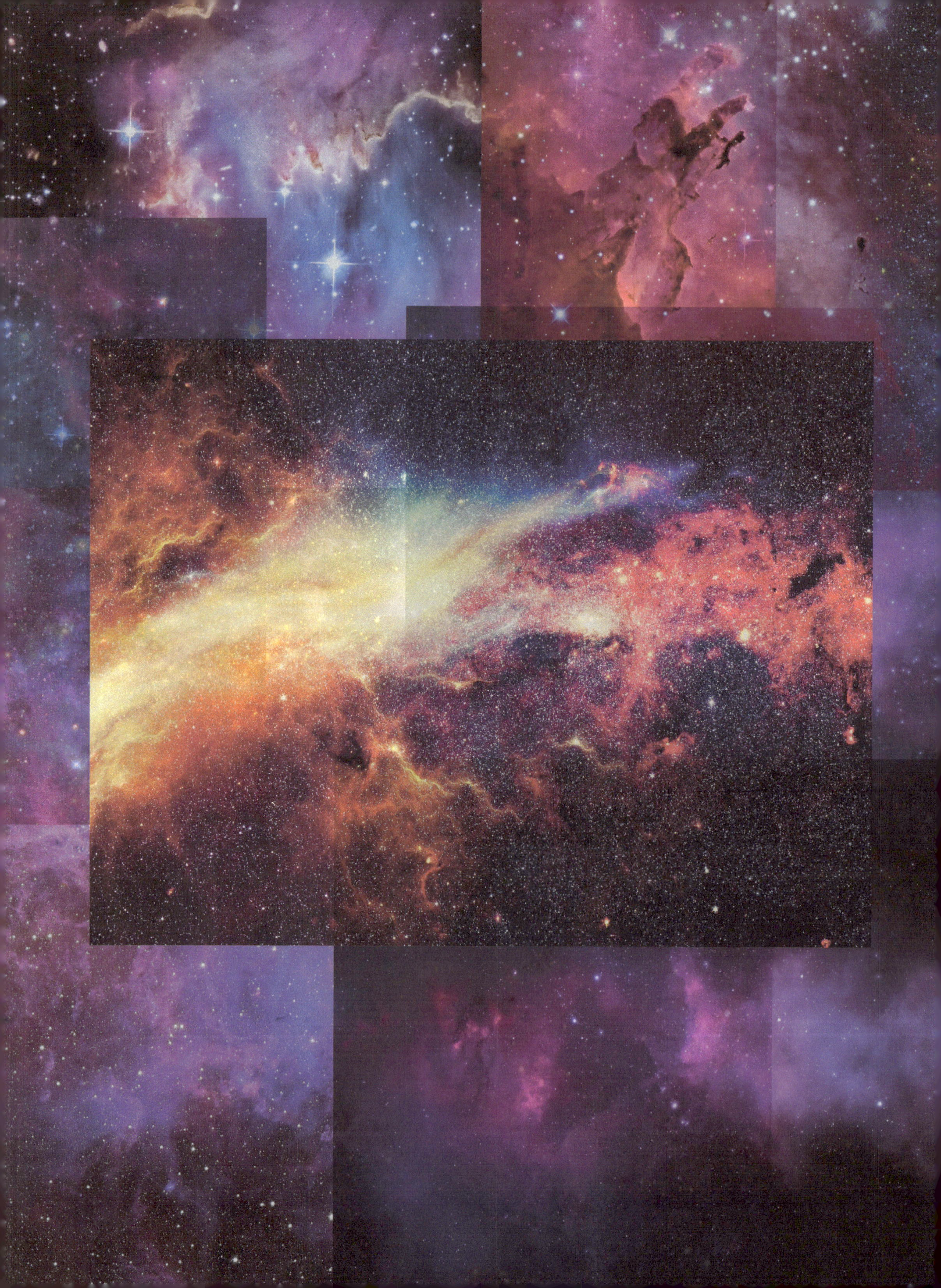

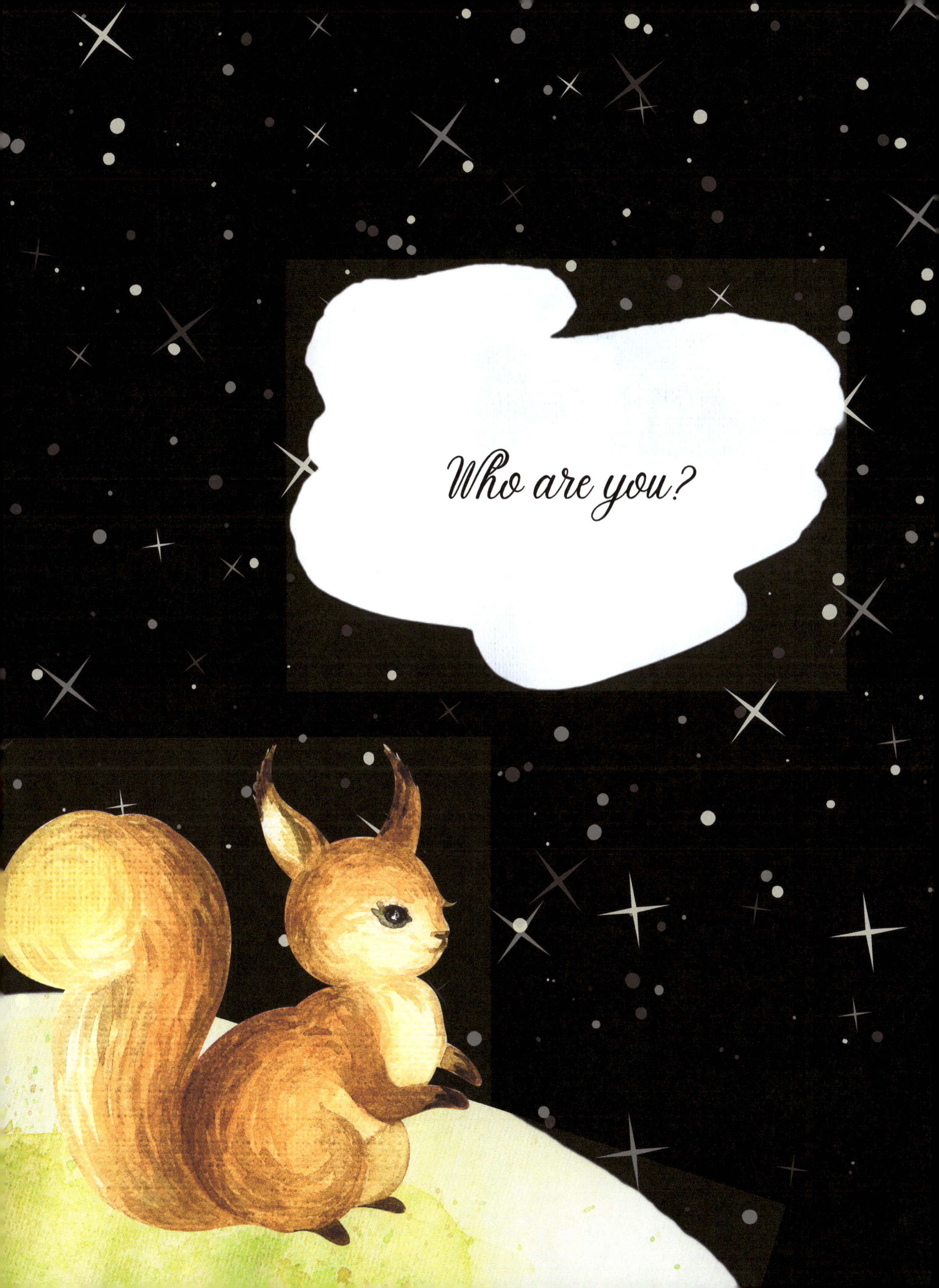
Who are you?

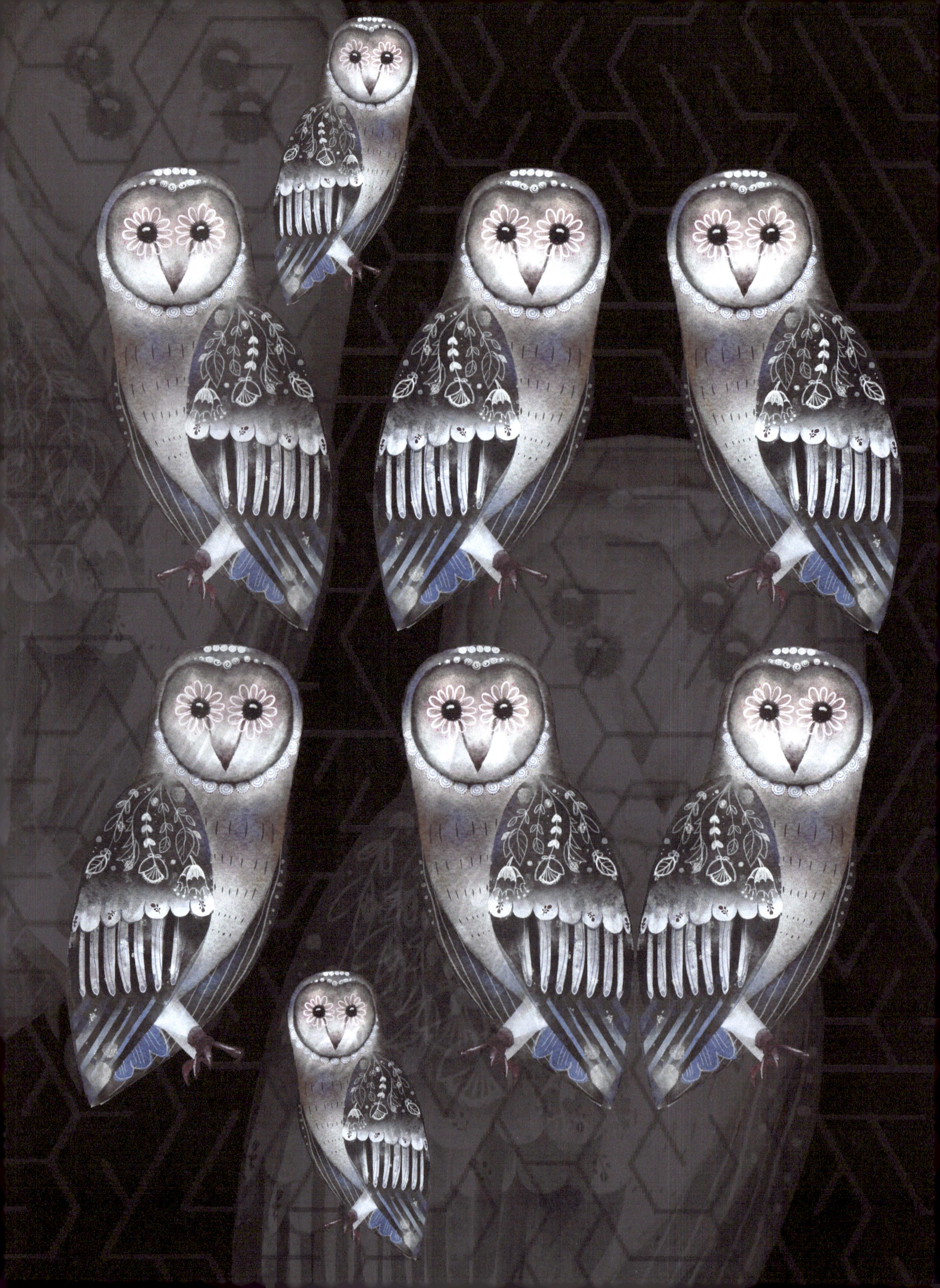

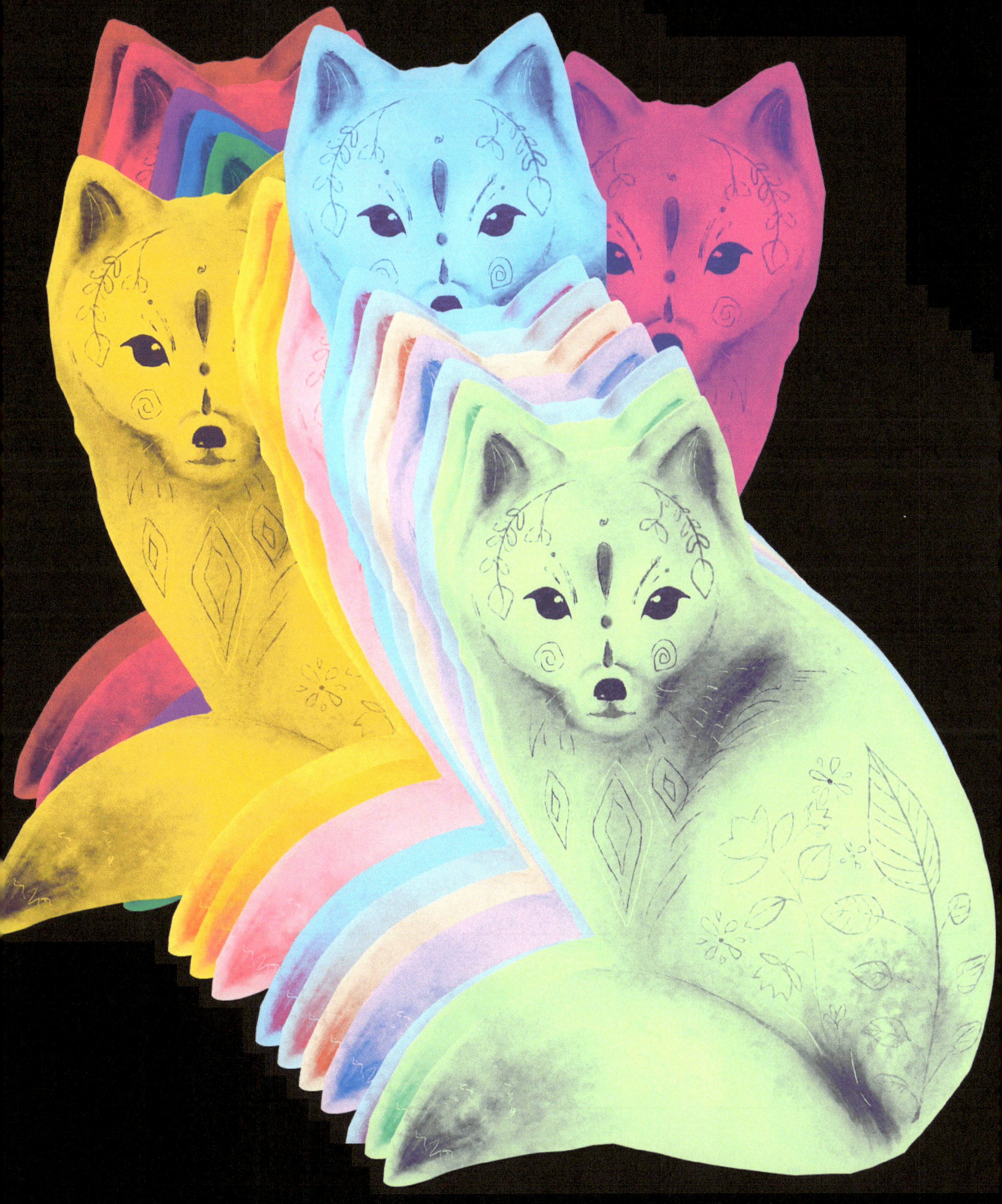

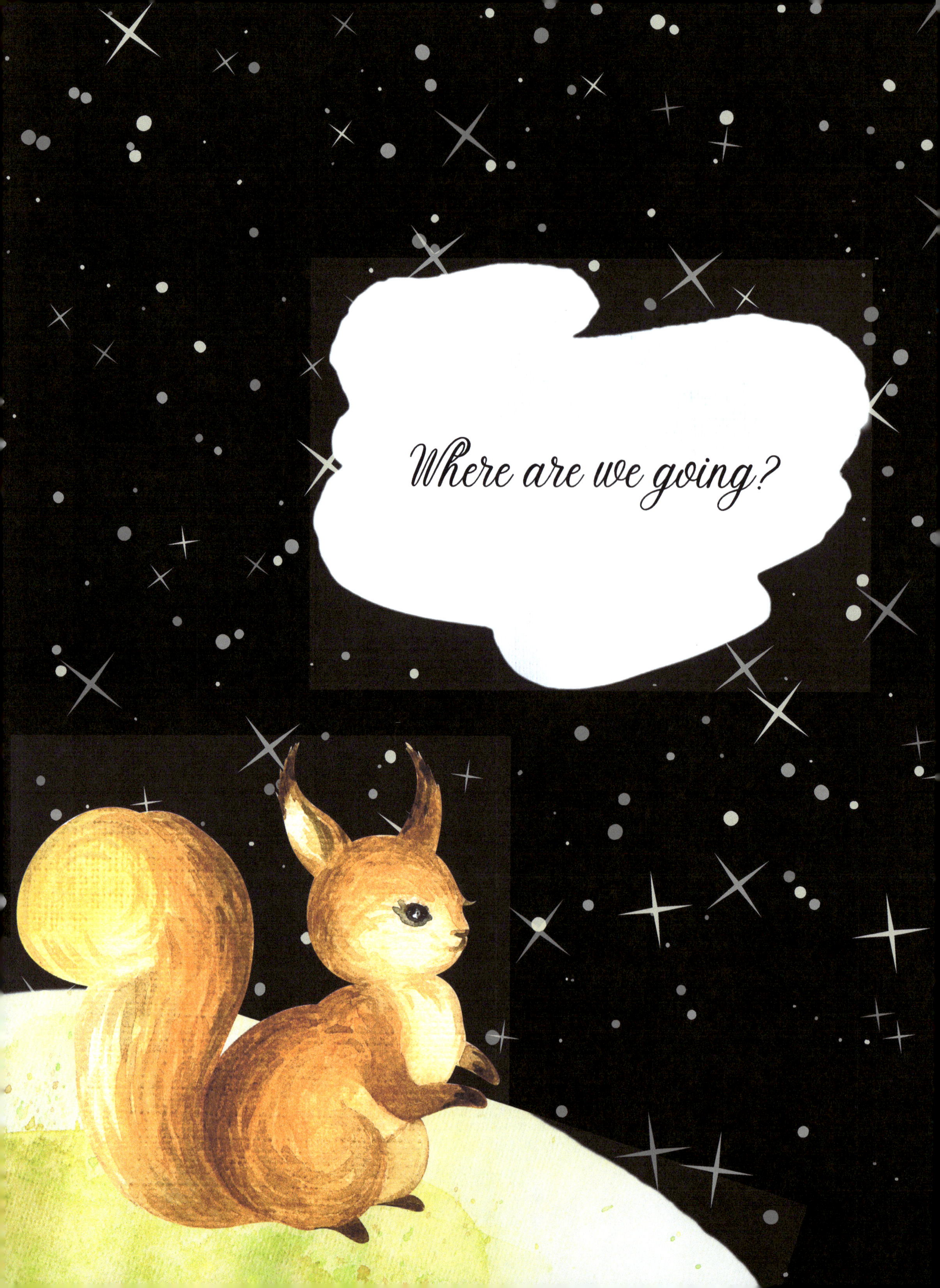
Where are we going?

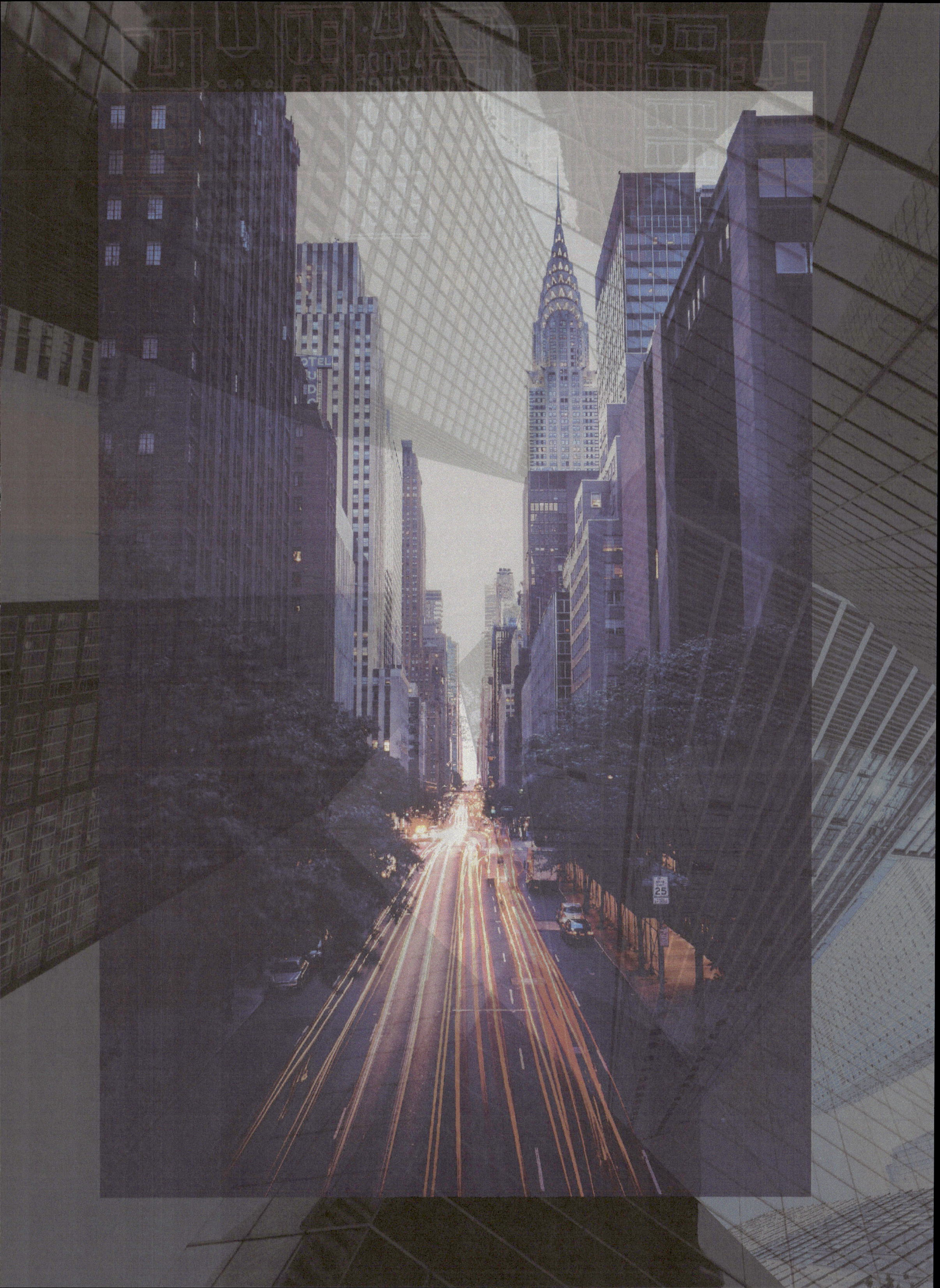
25

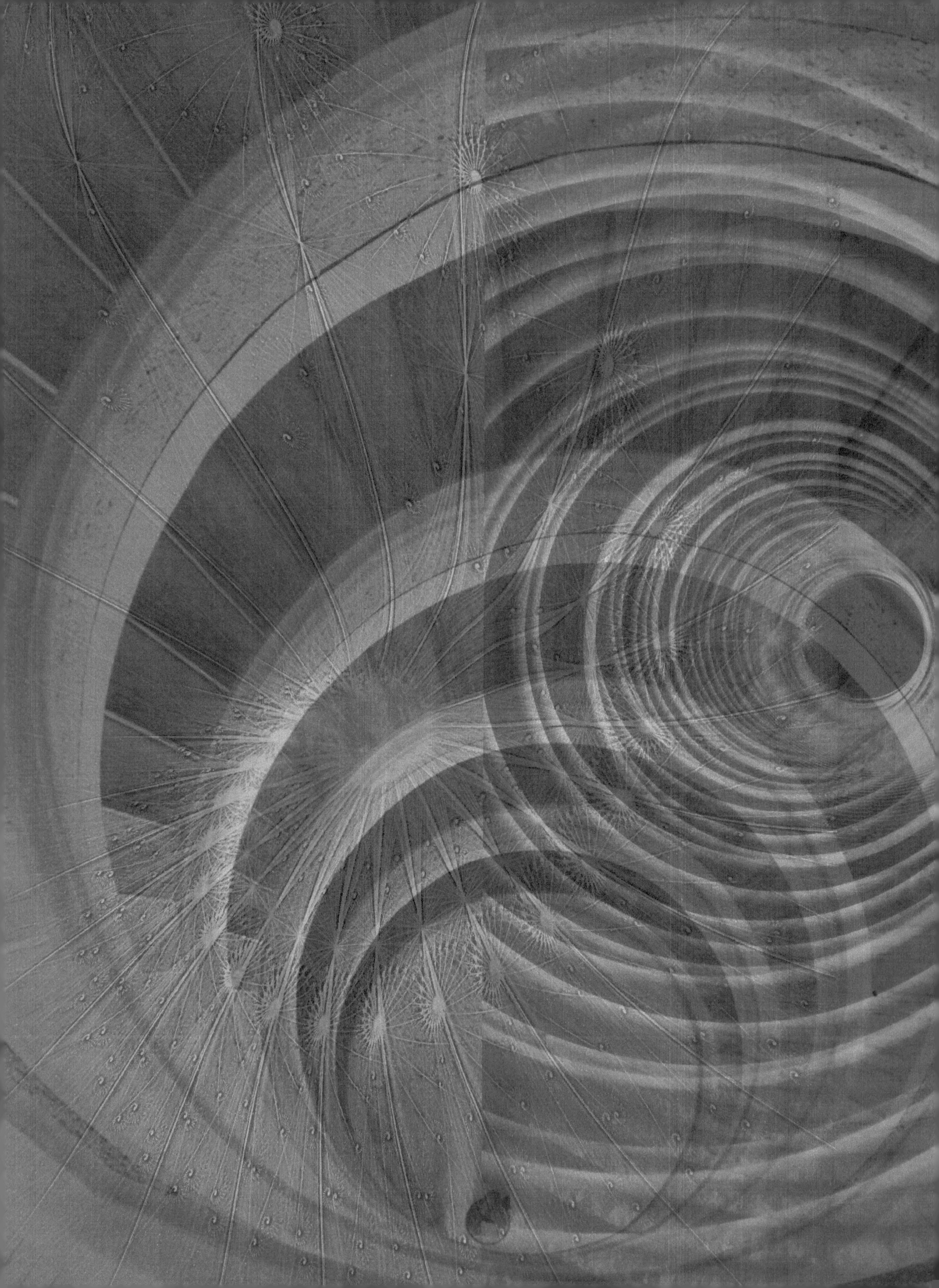

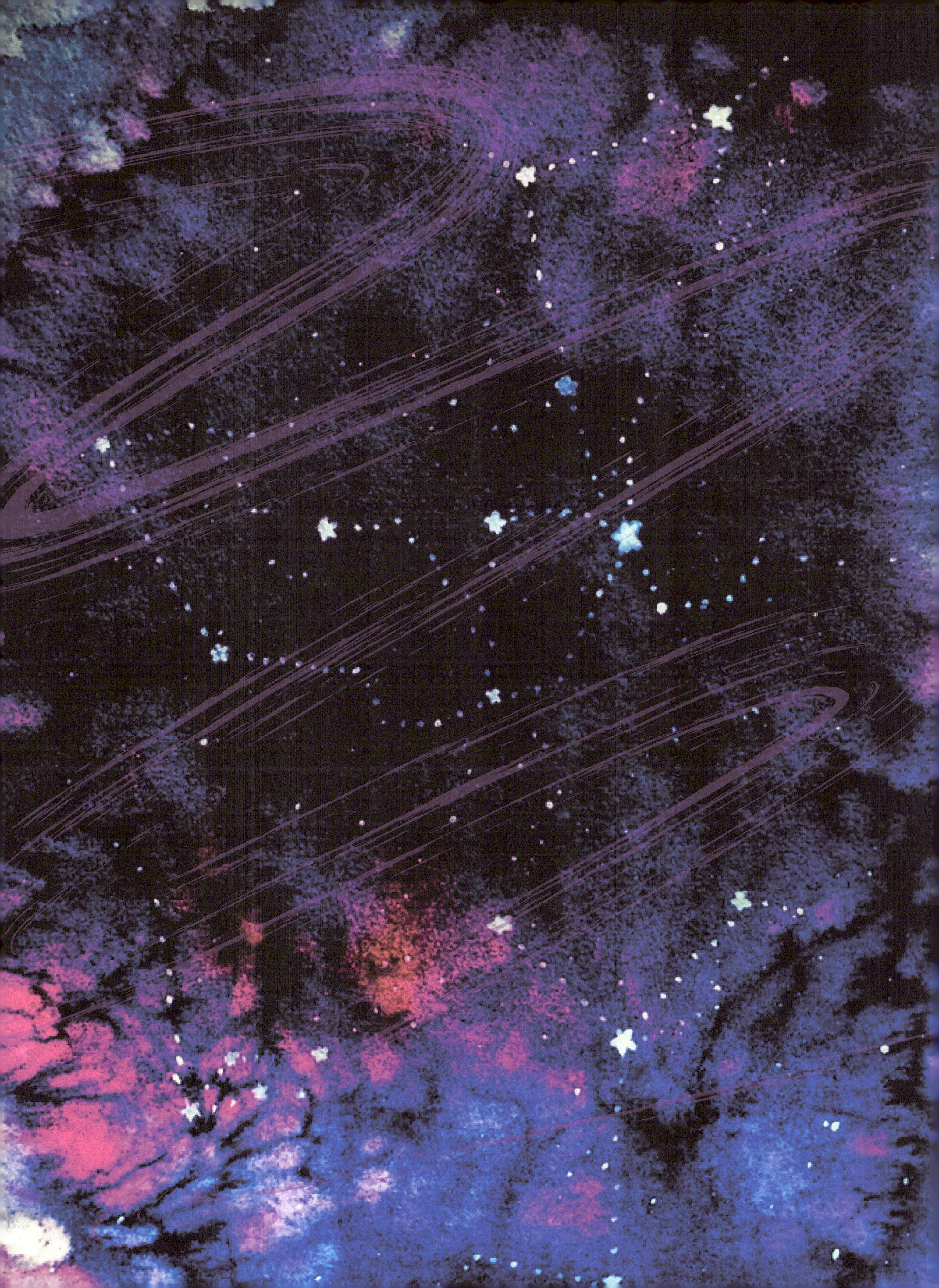

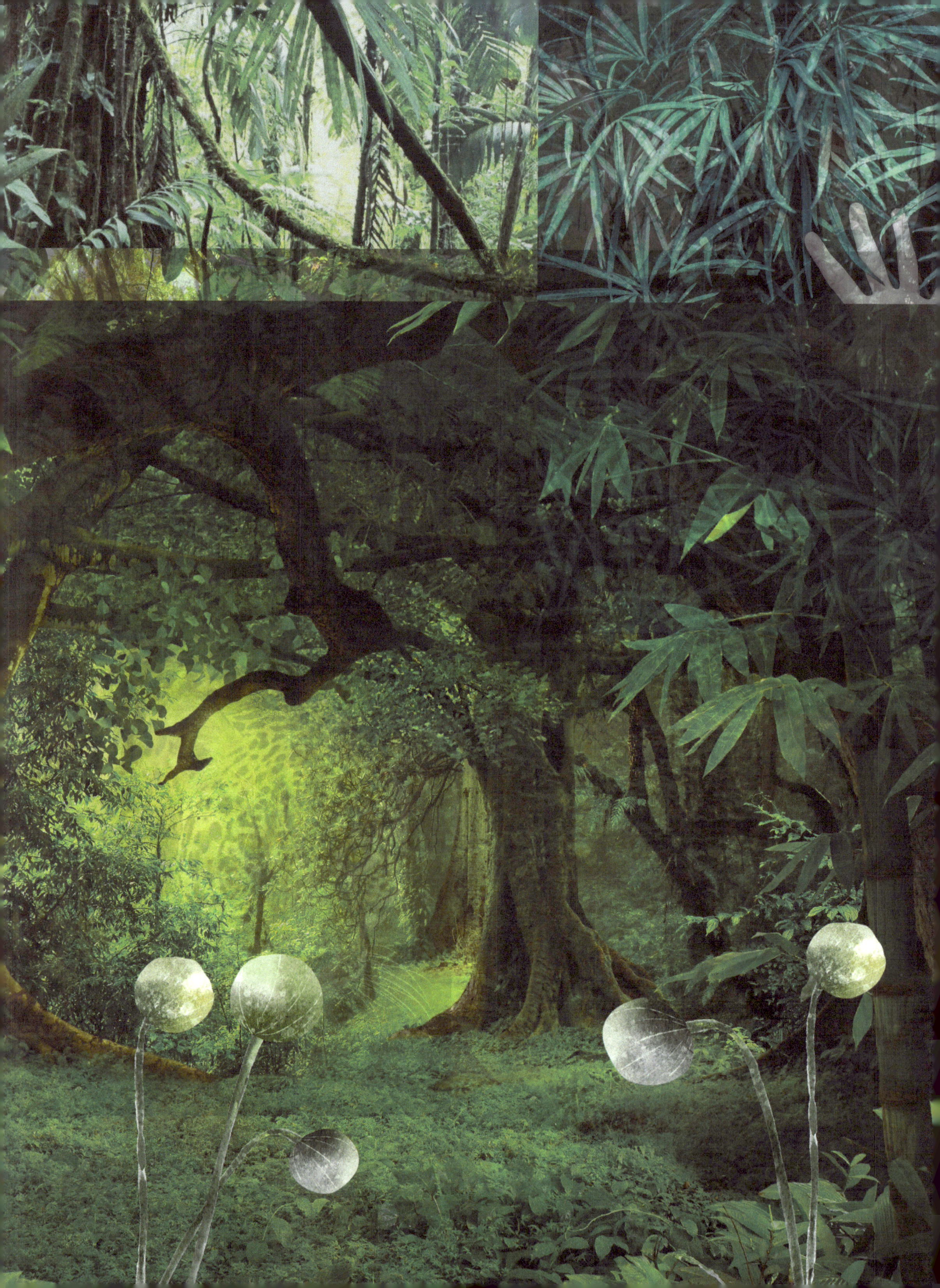

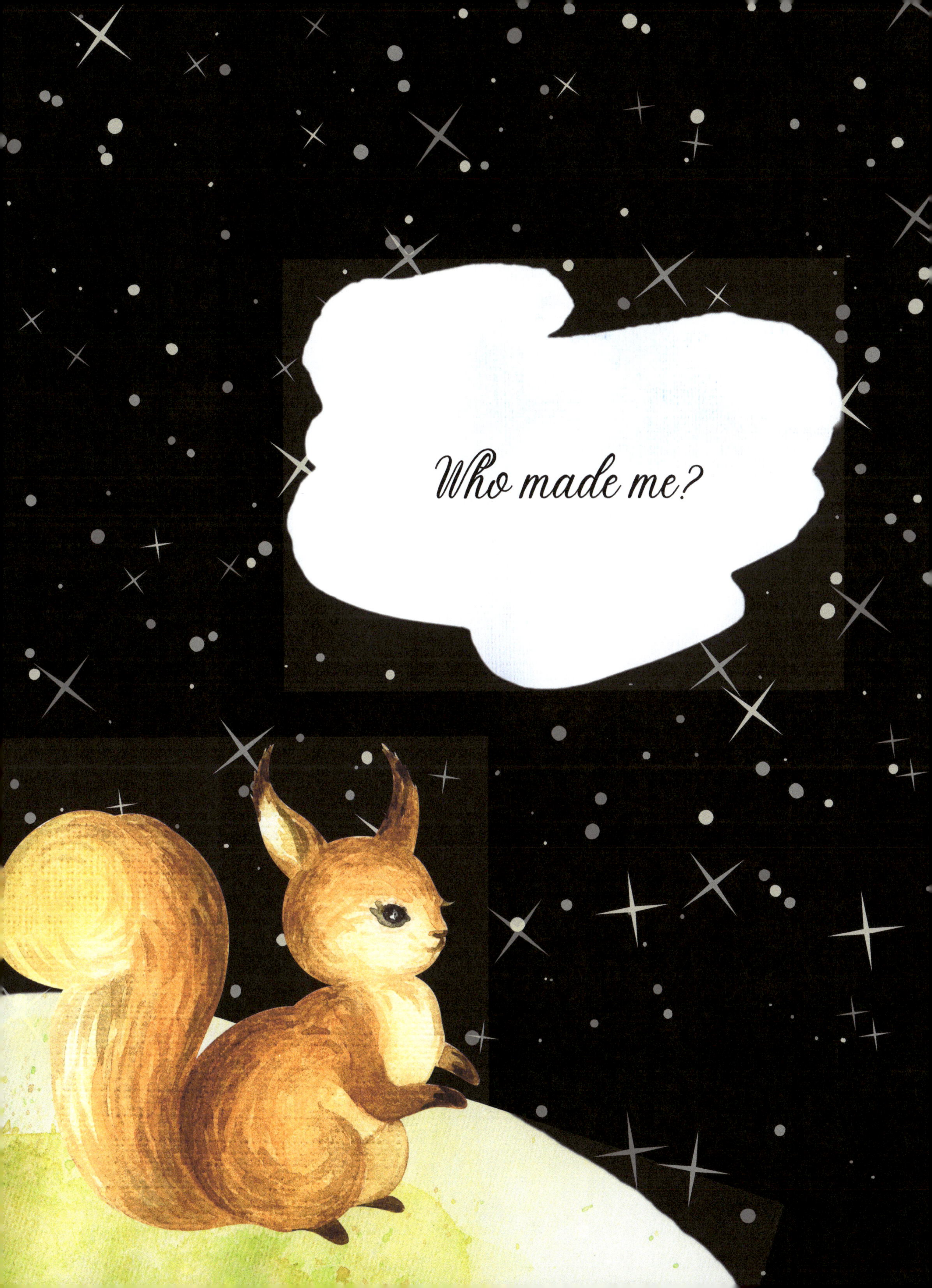
Who made me?

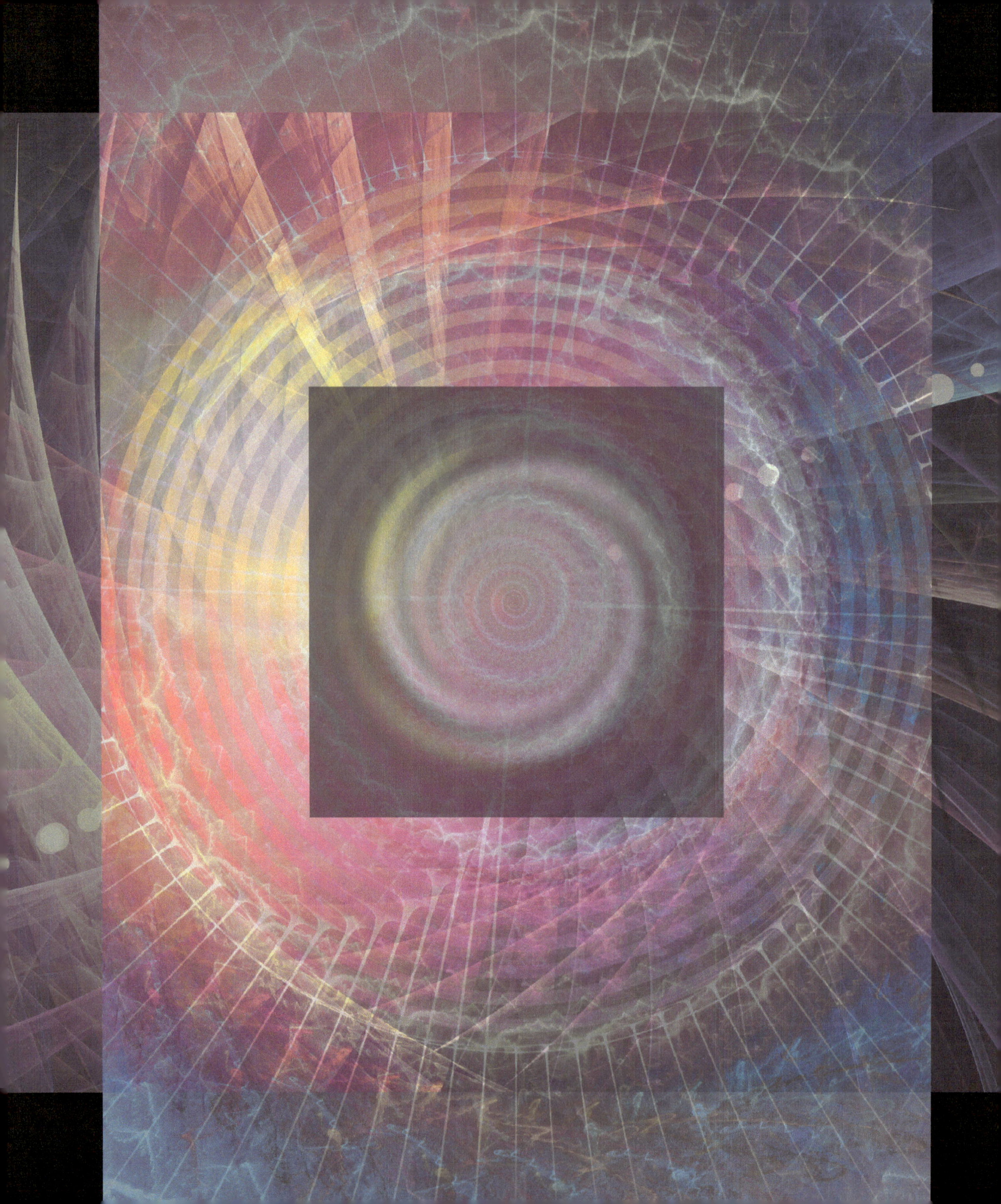

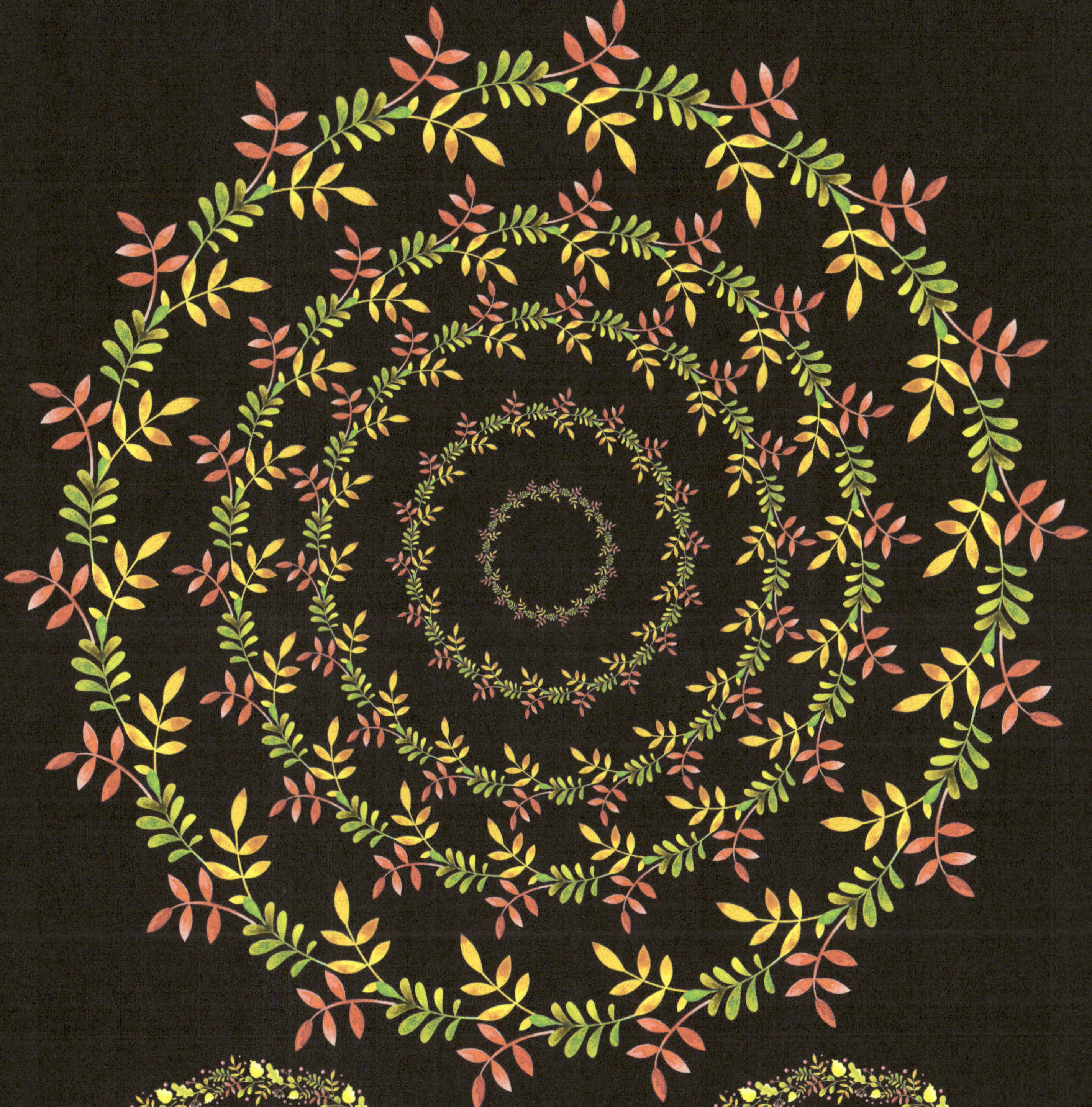
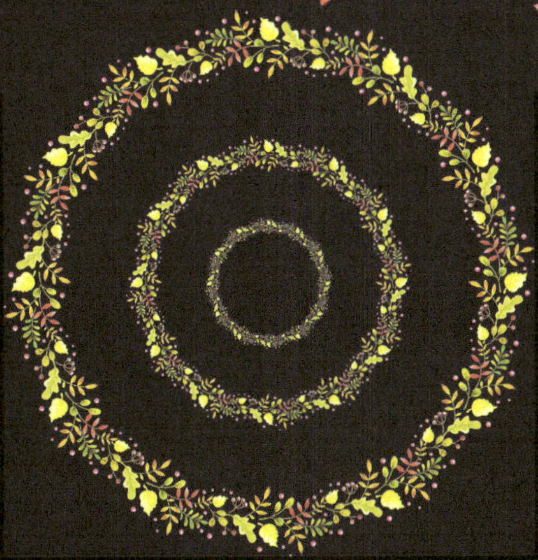
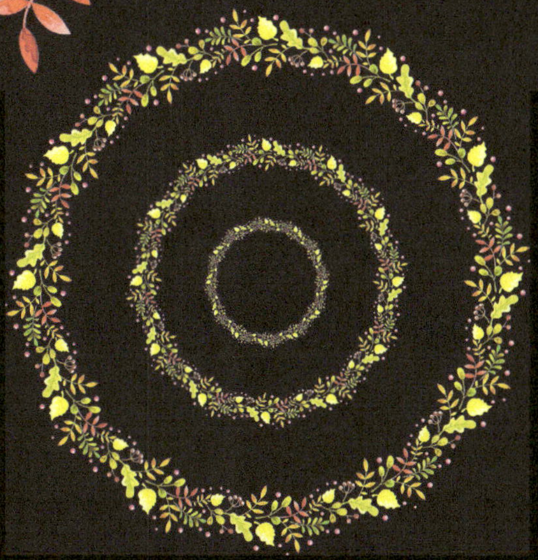

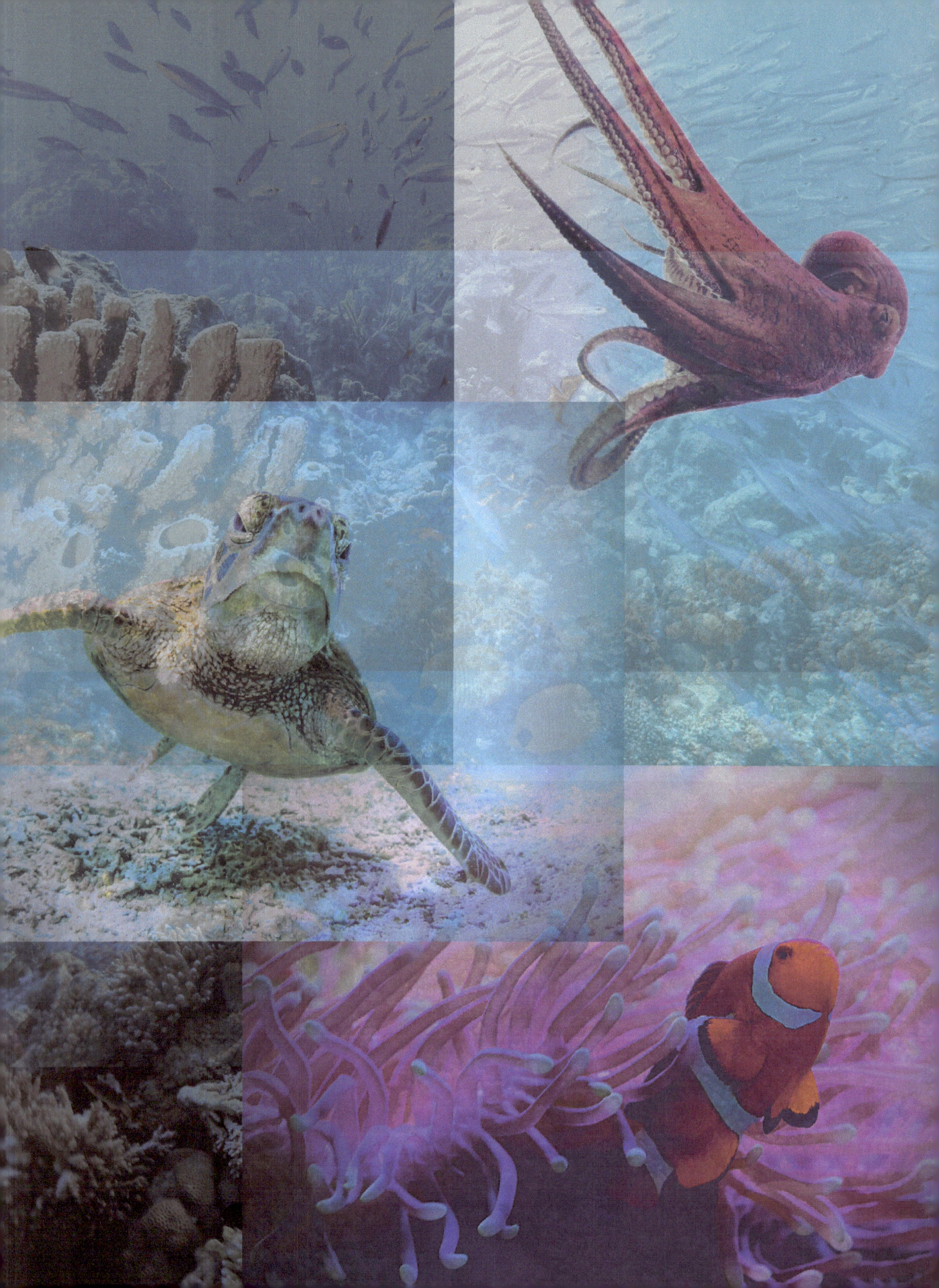

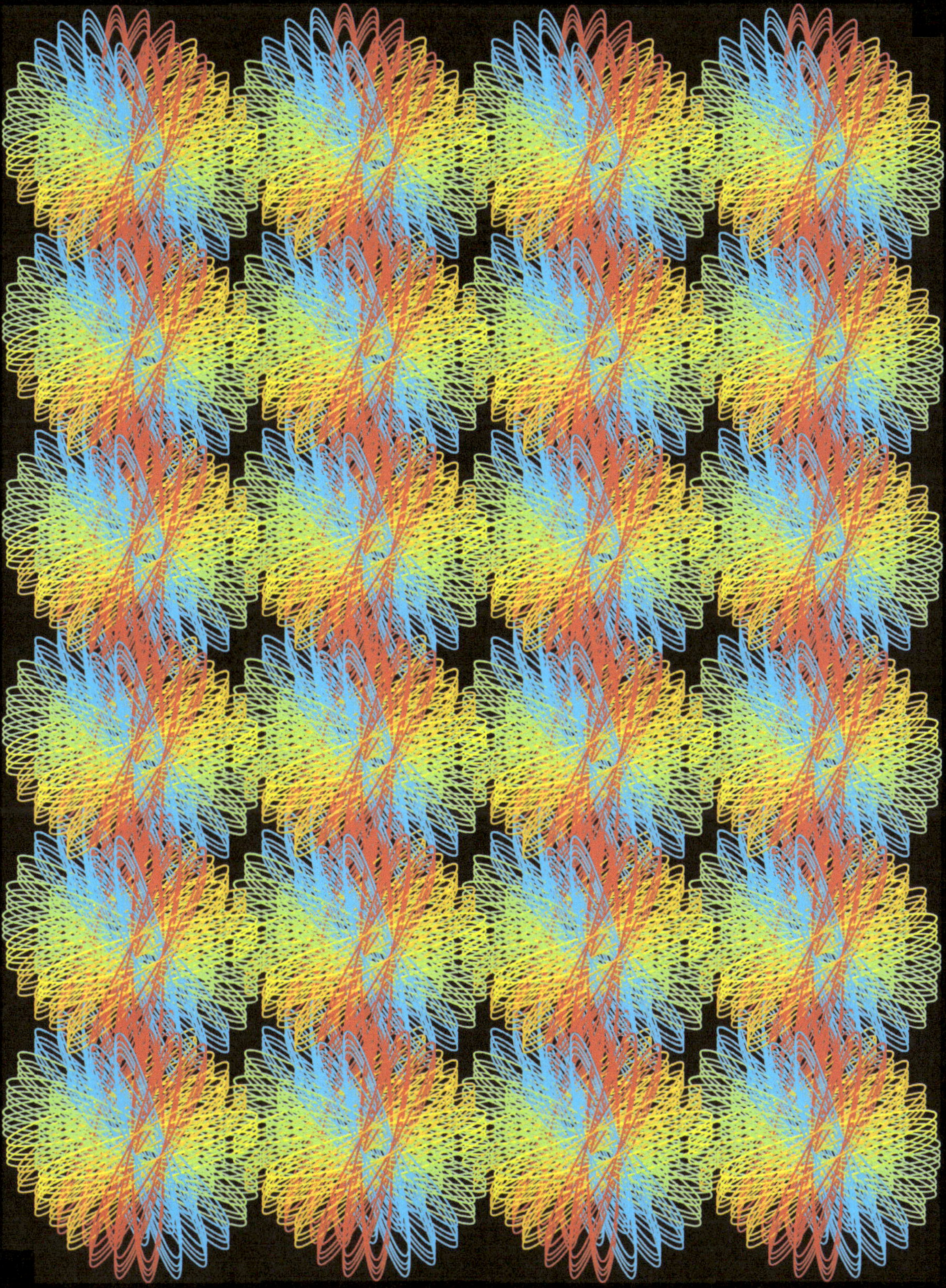

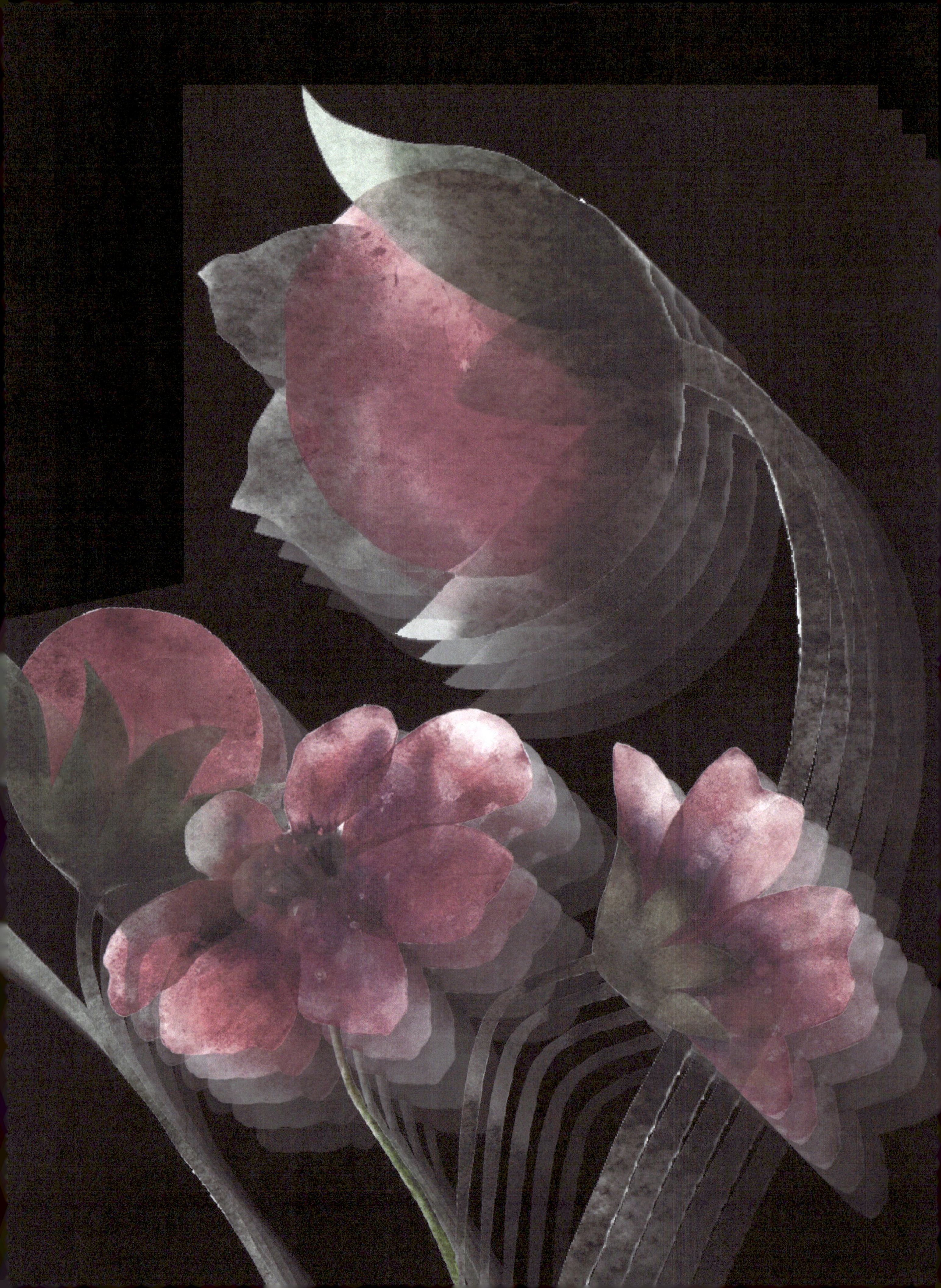

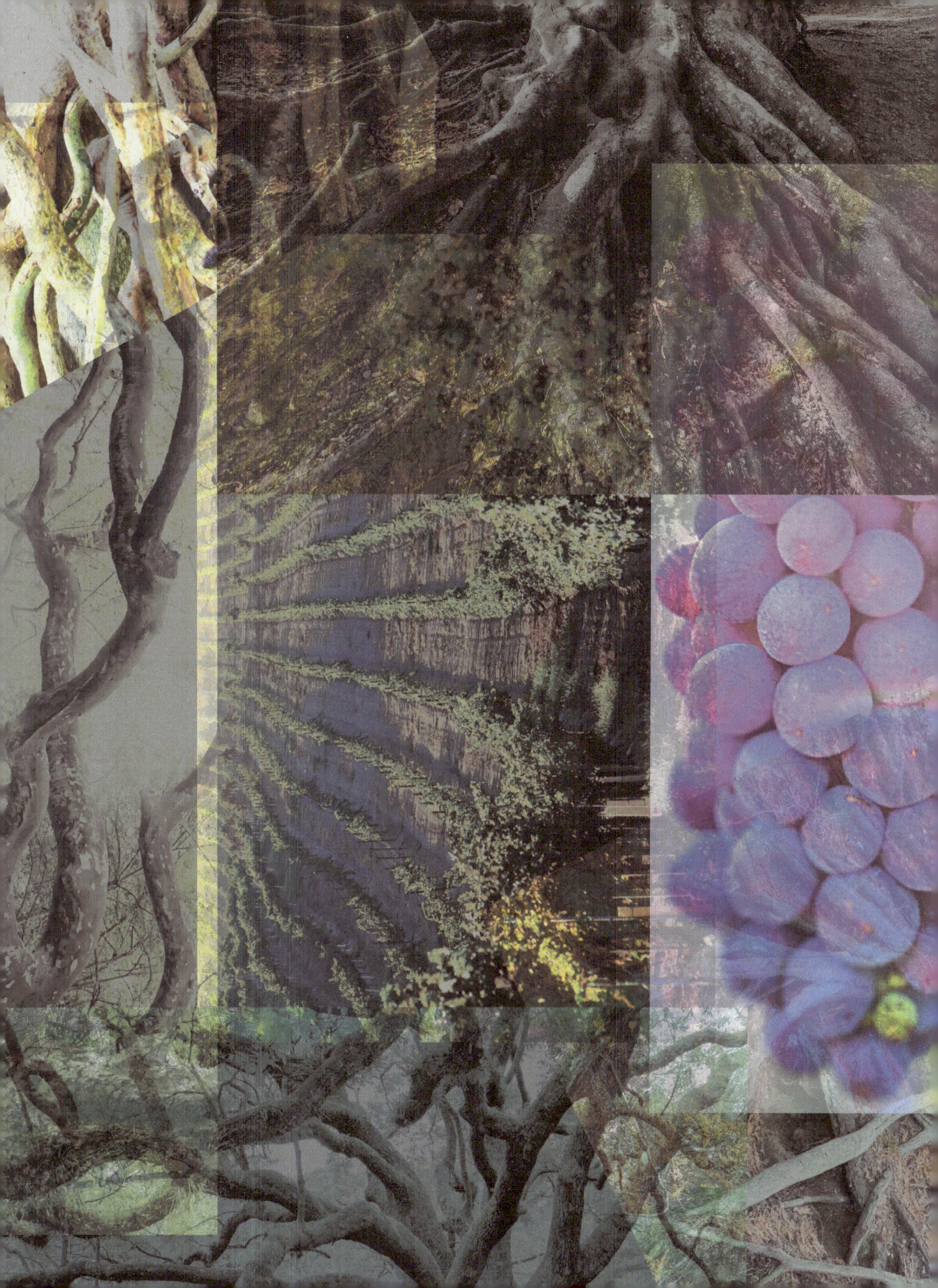

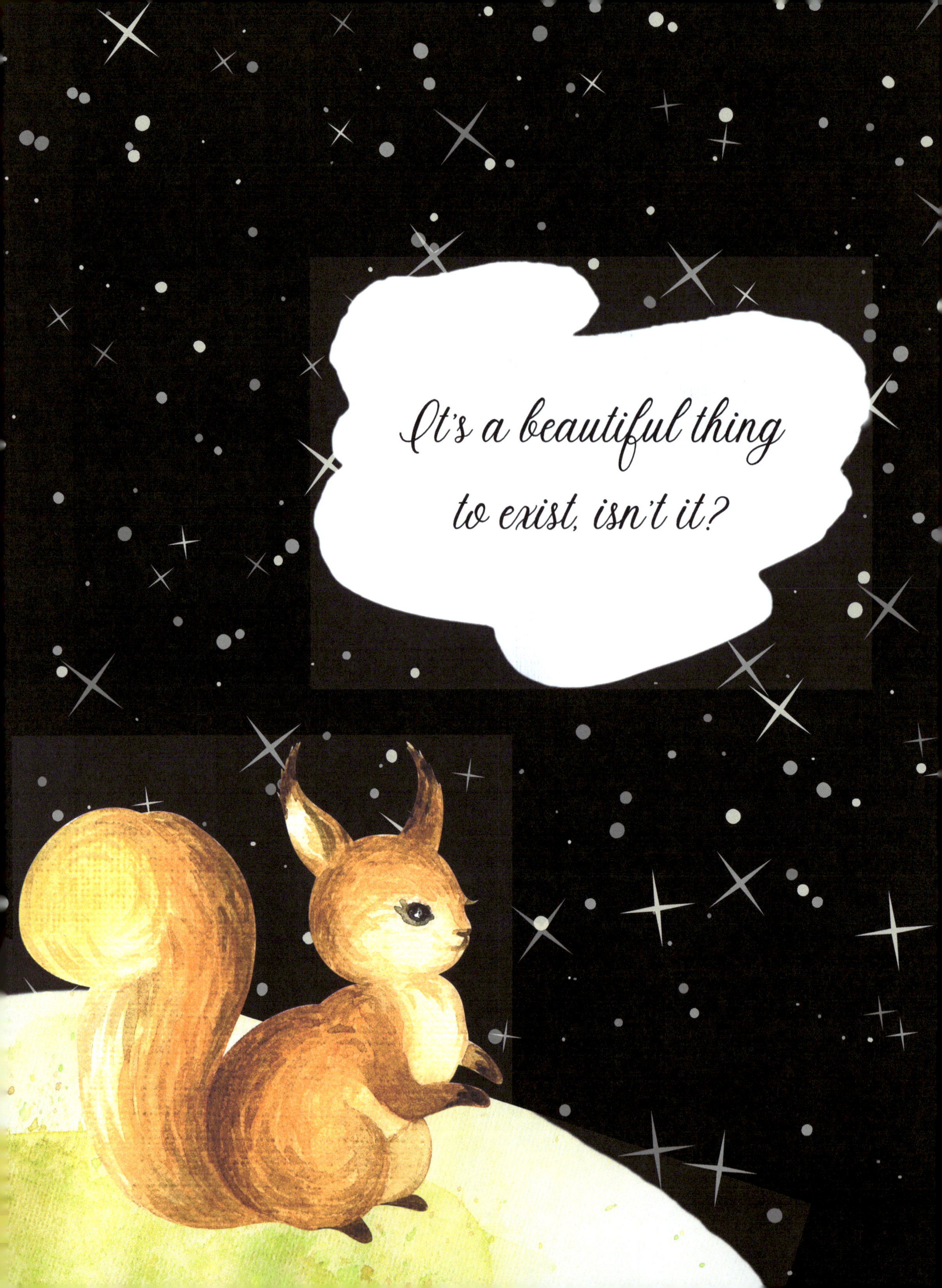
It's a beautiful thing to exist, isn't it?

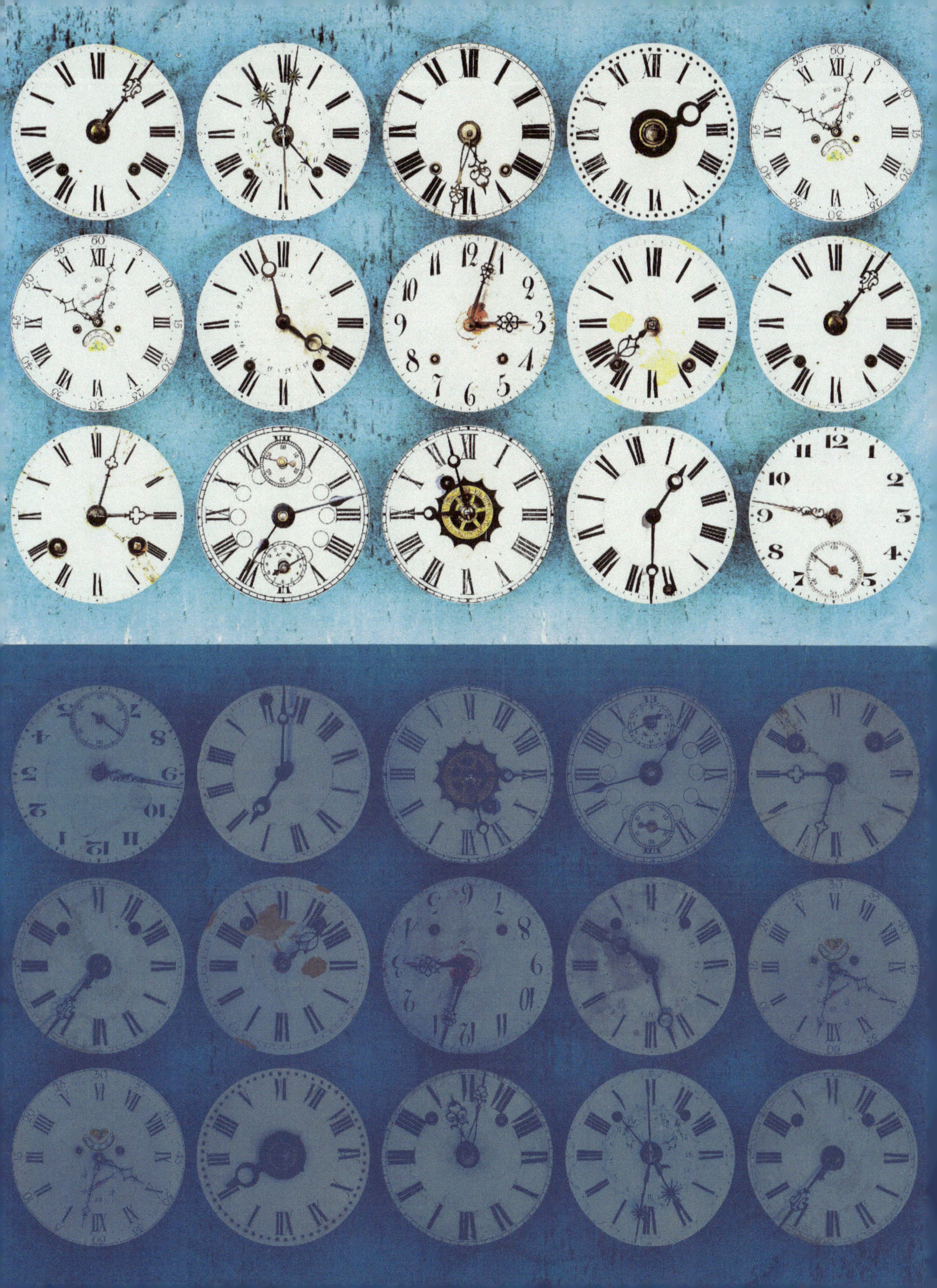

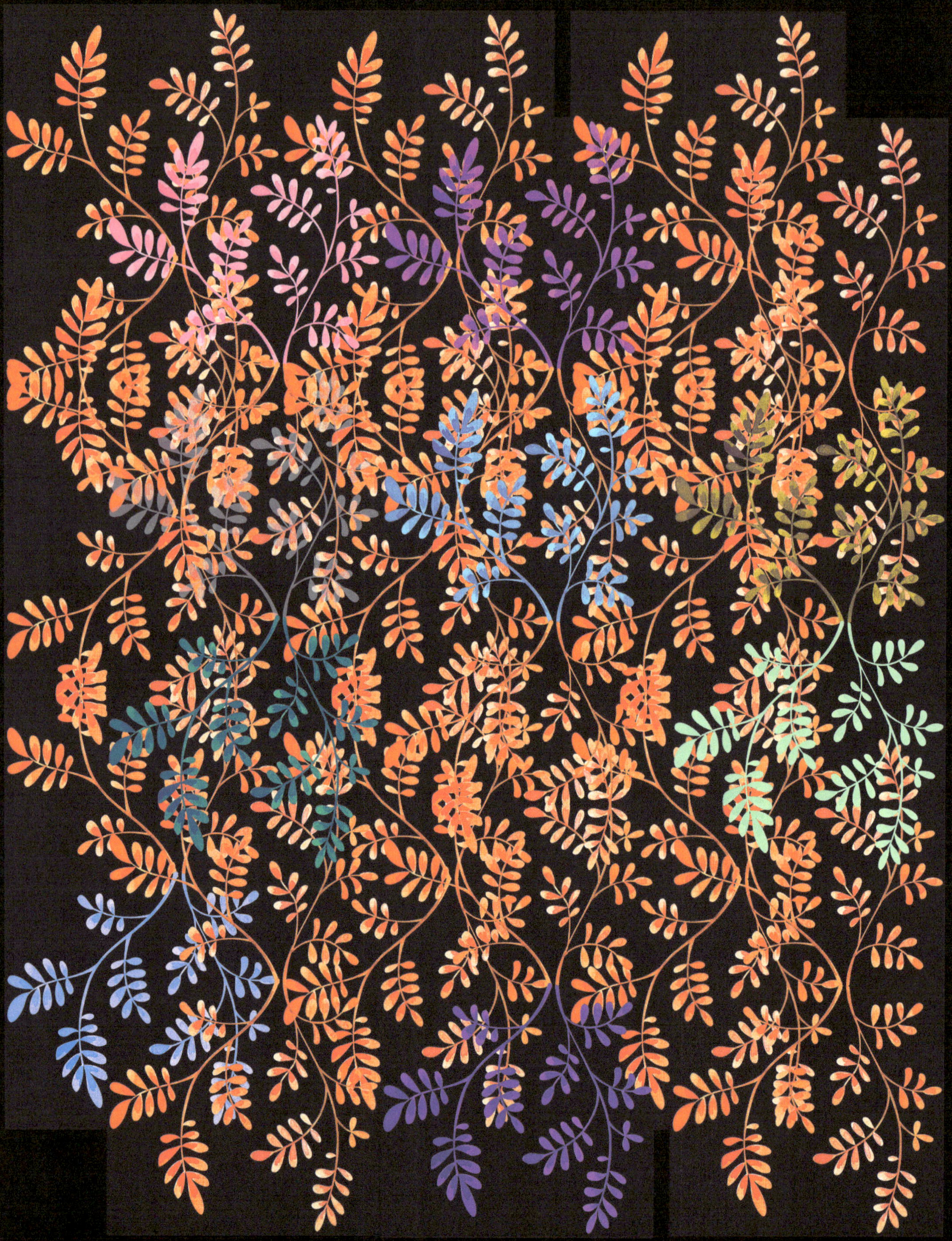

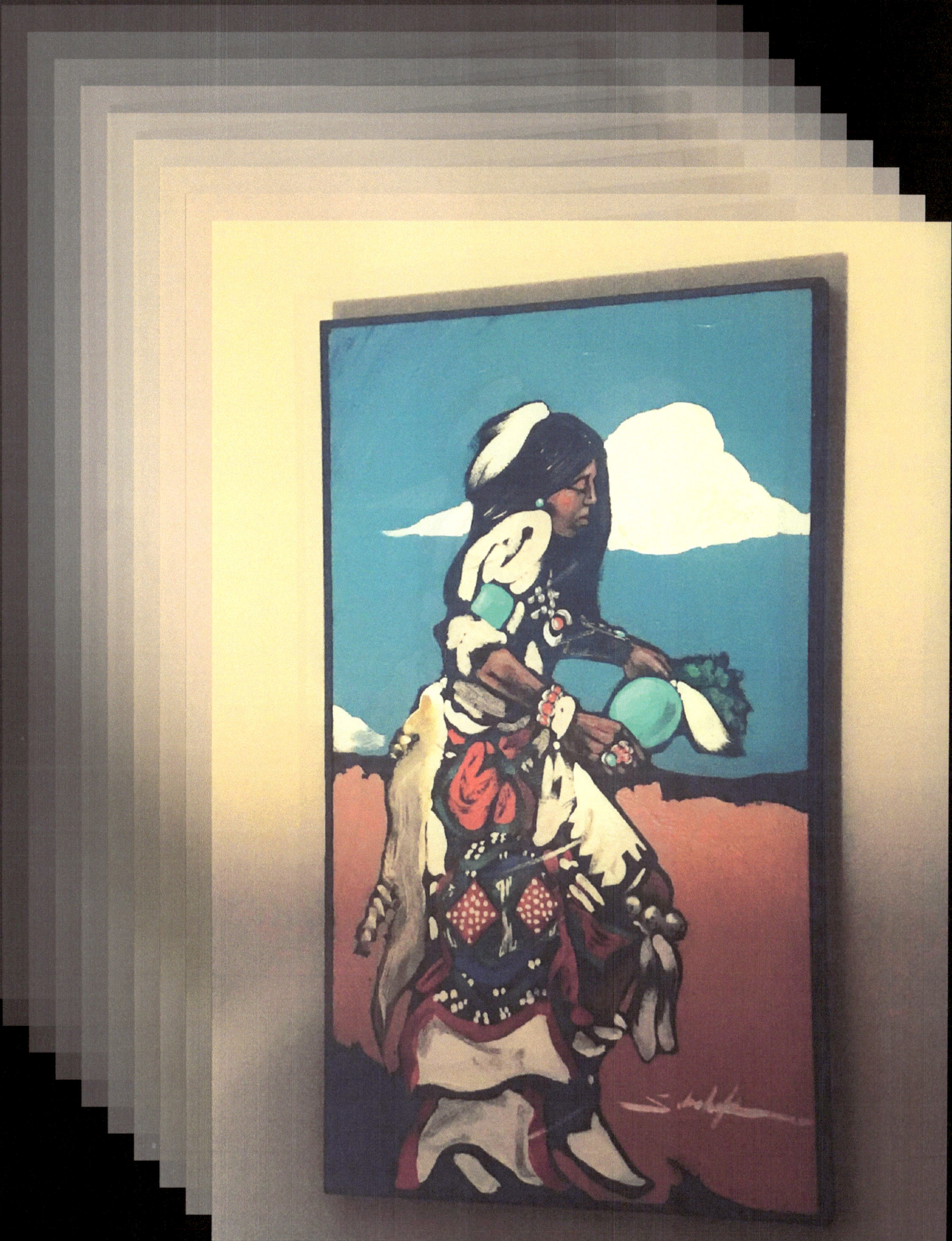

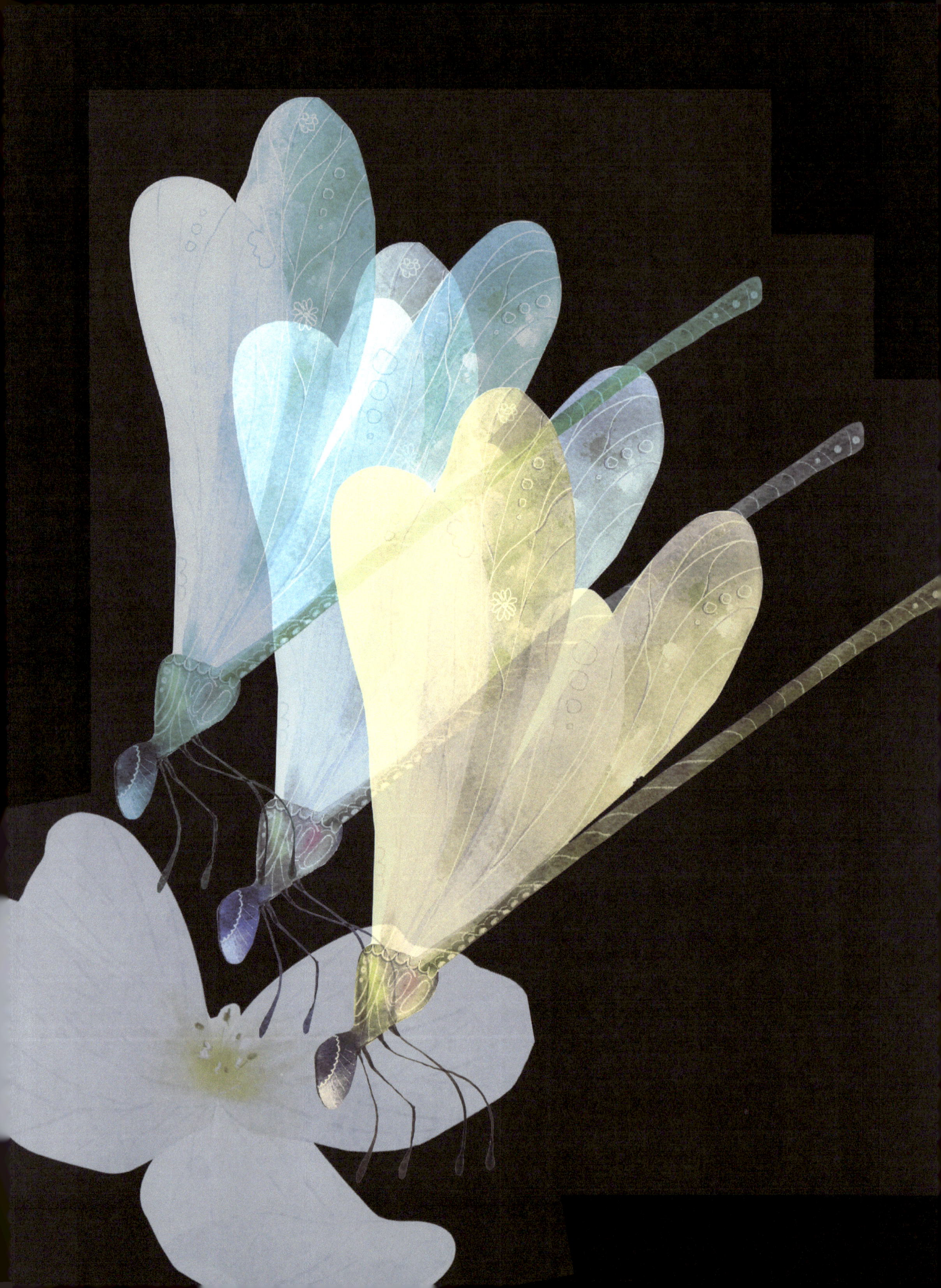

I'll see you
on the other side.

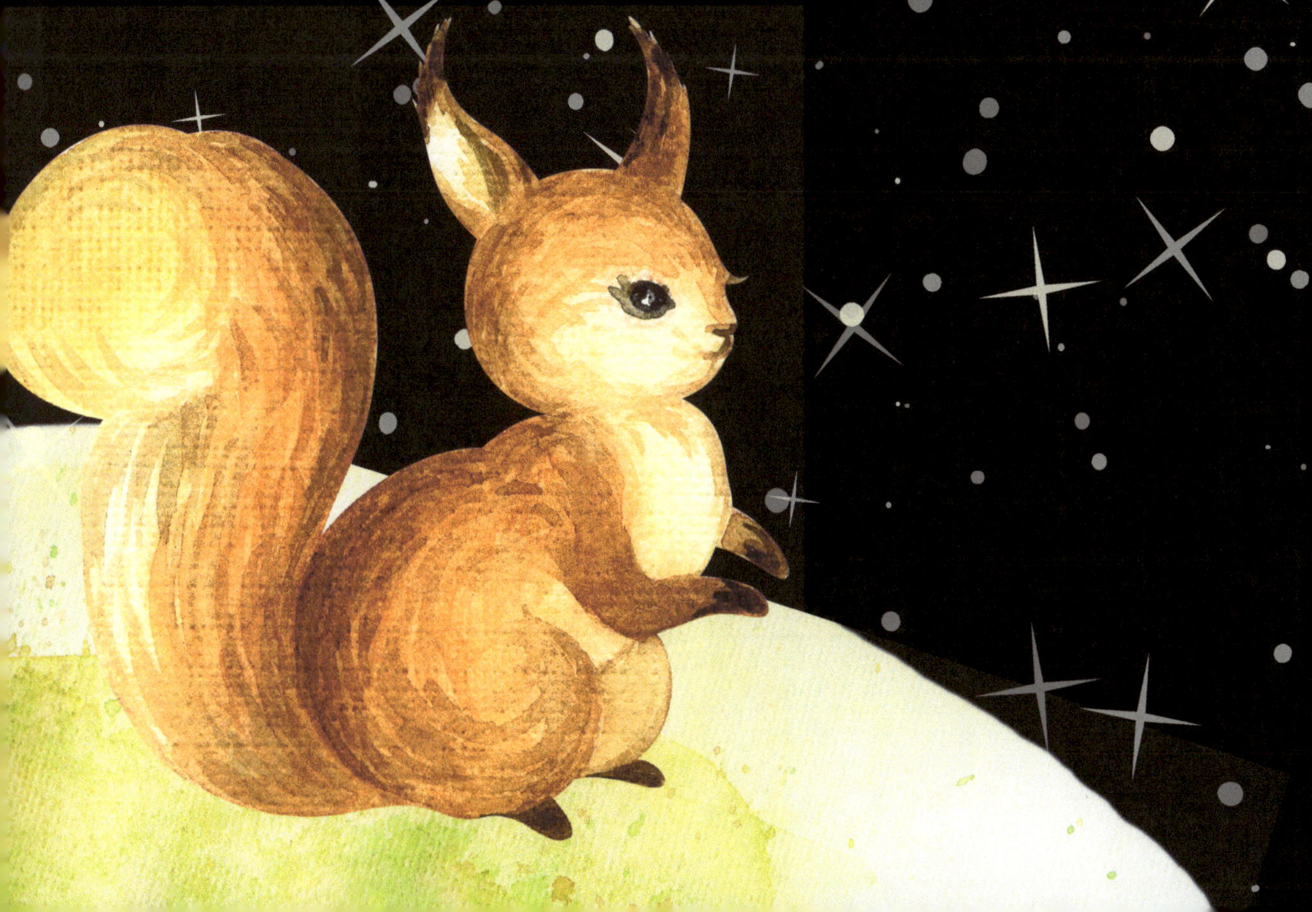

www.ingramcontent.com/pod-product-compliance
Lightning Source LLC
Chambersburg PA
CBHW051823210526
45473CB00005B/1720
* 9 7 9 8 5 4 5 4 7 2 9 9 4 *